ALL AMERICAN STORIES

C. G. DRAPER

Longman

All American Stories B

Pearson Education, 10 Bank Street, White Plains, NY 10606

Vice president, primary and secondary editorial: Ed Lamprich
Senior development editor: Lauren Weidenman
Production editor: Lynn Contrucci
Senior art director: Elizabeth Carlson
Vice president, marketing: Kate McLoughlin
Senior manufacturing buyer: Edith Pullman
Cover design: Lissi Sigillo
Cover art: Horatio Shaw (1847–1918). Barnyard in Winter. Ca. 1885–1890. Smithsonian
    American Art Museum, Washington, DC. Photo from Smithsonian American Art Museum,
    Washington, DC/Art Resource, New York
Text design: Elizabeth Carlson
Text composition: Rainbow Graphics
Text fonts: Franklin Gothic Book and Minion
Illustrations: John Edens: "The Romance of a Busy Broker"; Tom LaPadula: "A Jury of Her
    Peers" and "The Whale Hunt"; Rob Lawson: "The Story of an Hour"; Isidre Mones: "The
    Ingrate"; Tim Otis: "Paste"; Gonzalez Vicente: "The Lost Phoebe"

Library of Congress Cataloging-in-Publication Data

All American stories / [edited] by C.G. Draper.
     p. cm.
  Includes index.
  ISBN 0-13-192988-7
  1. English language—Textbooks for foreign speakers. 2. Short stories,
American—Adaptations. 3. Readers (Secondary) I. Draper, C. G.
PE1128.A365 2006
428.6′4—dc22

            2004026234

LONGMAN ON THE **WEB**

Longman.com offers online resources for
teachers and students. Access our Companion
Websites, our online catalog, and our local
offices around the world.

Visit us at **longman.com**.

Printed in the United States of America
3 4 5 6 7 8 9 10—ML—09 08 07 06

Contents

To the Student

The stories in this book were written many years ago by seven of America's most famous writers. Some words and sentences in their stories have been changed. These changes make the stories easier to understand for students learning English as a second language. The stories begin at the lower intermediate level of English language proficiency and end at the upper intermediate level.

The introductory unit—"What Is a Short Story?"—is different from Units 1 to 6. It will help you understand how to read a short story. It explains the terms **characters, plot, setting,** and **theme.** It also points out details about these features as it takes you through a story called "The Story of an Hour," by Kate Chopin.

In Units 1 to 6, you will find:

- A paragraph about the life of the person who wrote the story.

- A section called "Before You Read." This section introduces you to the story. It gives you important background information. And it tells you the meaning of some words that are important in the story.

- The story itself and pictures that help you understand the story.

- A section called "After You Read." This section contains reading comprehension questions, discussion questions, and an extension activity. It also includes exercises in vocabulary and word study, and gives you practice in writing. In addition, this section gives you activities to help you understand the elements of literature.

Reading this book will help you improve many English language skills: reading, speaking, listening, and writing. You will also learn many things about American history and about the daily life of the country's people many years ago.

Good luck, and good reading!

What Is a Short Story?

Not all short stories are truly *short.* Some are many pages long. But all short stories have certain things in common: **characters, plot, setting,** and **theme.** These are the elements of a short story.

Characters are the people or the animals in a story. A good writer creates characters that you care about. You read the story to find out what happens to them.

The **plot** of the story is what happens to the characters. Things that happen are called events. Sometimes the events really happened. Often the events are the author's creation.

The **setting** is where and when the story happens. In some stories, the setting is very specific. For example, a story about the first modern Olympic Games would probably be set in Athens, Greece, in the year 1896.

The **theme** is a general idea about life that the author conveys by telling the story. Some stories do not have a theme.

The model story is "The Story of an Hour" by Kate Chopin. Here are the characters, plot, setting, and theme of the story.

Characters
Louise Mallard, a married woman; Josephine, her sister; Richards, a friend; Brently Mallard, Louise's husband

Plot
A woman finds out that her husband has died suddenly. Her feelings about his death change with time.

Setting
Time: No time is given, but the story was written in 1894.
Place: Louise's house

Theme
The need for freedom is sometimes greater than the need for love.

Character

Authors have many ways to help you get to know their characters. They can describe what a character looks like. They can tell you the character's thoughts and feelings. They can tell you what the character does and says. It is easier to believe in characters that seem real.

The main character is the most important character in the story. Often, the main character changes as a result of what happens in the story. The change the character goes through is usually important. It can be important both to the character's life and to the meaning of the story.

In "The Story of an Hour," the main character is Louise Mallard. At the beginning of the story she is described as having "a weak heart." Later, the author writes, "how strong and well she looked—so full of joy." What you know about a character at the start of a story can change by the story's end.

Plot

The plot is the action—what happens. The plot is made up of events that are connected to one another. In most cases, the author tells you about these events in the order in which they happened. You keep reading the story to find out what happens next.

Often there is conflict, or a problem, in a short story. The conflict could be a disagreement between two characters. It could be a struggle between a person and a part of nature, such as the weather. The conflict could even be between two different feelings within a person.

In "The Story of an Hour," Louise Mallard's problem is that her feelings are in conflict. Louise's problem is solved at the end of the story in a most surprising way.

Setting

A story's setting is its place and time. Place might be a country or a room in a building. Time might be the season or the time of day. Authors can tell you the setting directly. They can also tell you indirectly, giving you information such as how people are dressed or what is happening in the world.

Some stories can only happen in a specific setting. Other stories can take place anywhere, at any time. Many fairy tales have the same imaginary setting: "once upon a time" in a "faraway land."

"The Story of an Hour" takes place in Louise Mallard's home. These words tell you that it is spring: "The air smelled like spring rain. . . . Birds sang near the house." You can assume the year is around 1894 because the story was written in that year, and the action takes place in the present time.

Theme

The theme is the central idea or message an author conveys by telling the story. The idea can usually be expressed as a general statement about life.

Some authors tell you the theme directly. However, most authors would prefer that you figure out the theme after you have read the story. You might need to think about the story or reread certain parts before you can put the theme into words.

Figuring out a story's theme can help you understand the story better and enjoy it more. You need to understand a story well before you can put its theme into words. And understanding a story is a big part of enjoying it.

The theme of "The Story of an Hour" is that the need for freedom is sometimes more powerful than the need for love.

The Story of an Hour

Adapted from the story by Kate Chopin

Plot: The first paragraph sets the plot in motion. The reader learns that the main character has a weak heart and that her husband has just died.

They knew that Louise Mallard had a weak heart. So they broke the bad news softly. Her husband, Brently, was dead.

"There was a train accident, Louise," said her sister, Josephine, quietly.

Her husband's friend, Richards, stood with Josephine. Richards brought the news, but Josephine told the story. She spoke in broken sentences.

"Richards . . . was at the newspaper office. News of the accident came. Louise . . . Louise, Brently's name was on the list. Brently . . . was killed, Louise."

Character: Notice how Louise reacts to the news. First, she bursts into tears. Then, just as suddenly, she stops crying. The author compares her crying to a "sudden storm."

Louise did not hear the story coldly, like some other women would. She could not close her mind or her heart to the news. Like a sudden storm, her tears broke out. She cried loudly in her sister's arms. Then, just as suddenly, the tears stopped. She went to her room alone. She wanted no one with her.

In front of the window stood an empty chair. She sat down and looked out the window. She was very tired after her tears. Her body felt cold, her mind and heart were empty.

Setting: The story is set in Louise's home. It is spring. This is important because spring is a time of new beginnings. Louise doesn't feel it yet, but her husband's death could be a time of new beginnings for her.

Outside her window she could see the trees. The air smelled like spring rain. She could hear someone singing far away. Birds sang near the house. Blue sky showed between the clouds. She rested.

She sat quietly, but a few weak tears still fell. She had a young, strong face. But now her eyes showed nothing. She looked out the window at the blue sky. She was not thinking, or seeing. She was waiting.

There was something coming to her. She was waiting for it with fear. What was it? She did not know; she could not give it a name.

But she felt it coming out from the sky. It reached her through the sound, the smell, the color of the air.

Slowly she became excited. Her breath came fast, her heart beat faster. She began to see this thing. It wanted to find her and take her. She tried to fight against it. But she could not. Her mind was as weak as her two small white hands. Then she stopped fighting against it. A little word broke from her lips.

"Free," she said. "Free, free, free!" The emptiness and fear left her. Her eyes showed her excitement. Her heart beat fast, and the blood warmed her body. A sudden feeling of joy excited her.

She did not stop to ask if her joy was wrong. She saw her freedom clearly. She could not stop to think of smaller things.

She knew the tears would come again when she saw her husband's body. The kind hands, now dead and still. The loving face, now still and gray. But she looked into the future. She saw many long years to come that would belong to her alone. And now she opened her arms wide to those years in welcome.

There would be no one else to live for during those years. She would live for herself alone. There would be no strong mind above hers. Men and women always believe they can tell others what to do and how to think. Suddenly Louise understood that this was wrong. She could break away and be free of it.

And yet, she loved him—sometimes. Often she did not. What did love mean now? Now she understood that freedom is stronger than love.

"Free! Body and mind free!" she said again.

Her sister, Josephine, was waiting outside the door.

"Please open the door," Josephine cried. "You will make yourself sick. What are you doing in there, Louise? Please, please, let me in!"

"Go away. I am not sick." No, she was drinking in life through that open window.

She thought joyfully of all those days before her. Spring days, summer days. All kinds of days that would be her own. She began to hope life would be long. And just yesterday, life seemed too long!

Plot: Louise's heart beats fast as she discovers that she is free. The author tells you this fact twice. You already know that Louise has a weak heart. The author is giving you a clue about how the story will end. This is called **foreshadowing**.

Setting: This story was written in the 1890s. Women did not have much freedom at that time. For example, women did not yet have the right to vote in the United States. Think of how important personal freedom must have been to a woman like Louise.

The Story of an Hour   7

Character: Notice how much Louise's character has changed since the beginning of the story. She has changed from tired, cold, and empty to "full of joy."

Plot: The author surprises us with a twist in the plot. Brently Mallard is alive! What do you think will happen to Louise's freedom now?

Plot: Everyone thought Louise would die when she learned that her husband was dead. But what happened was the opposite—she died when she learned that her husband was alive. This is called **irony.**

After a while she got up and opened the door. Here eyes were bright, her cheeks were red. She didn't know how strong and well she looked—so full of joy. They went downstairs, where Richards was waiting.

A man was opening the door. It was Brently Mallard. He was dirty, and tired. He carried a suitcase and an umbrella. He was not killed in the train accident. He didn't even know there was an accident. He was surprised at Josephine's sudden cry. He didn't understand why Richards moved suddenly between them, to hide Louise from her husband.

But Richards was too late.

When the doctors came, they said it was her weak heart. They said she died of joy—of joy that kills. ✎

The Romance of a Busy Broker

Adapted from the story by O. Henry

About the Author

O. Henry was born in Greensboro, North Carolina, in 1862. His real name was William Sydney Porter. At the age of fifteen, he left school. He found work in a drugstore, a business office, a building designer's office, and finally a bank. When he was caught taking money from his own bank, O. Henry was arrested and put in prison for three years. While in prison, he published a book of adventure stories called *Cabbages and Kings*. In 1902, he moved to New York. It was there that he became famous for his short stories with surprise endings. He wrote hundreds of stories about the ordinary people of New York City. His most famous books include *The Four Million* and *The Voice of the City*. O. Henry died in 1910.

Before You Read

About "The Romance of a Busy Broker"

Characters
Harvey Maxwell, a stockbroker; Pitcher, a man who works for Harvey Maxwell; Miss Leslie, Harvey Maxwell's secretary

Plot
Maxwell is so busy that he doesn't remember having hired a new secretary the day before. And he doesn't remember another important event that happened.

Setting
Time: early 1900s
Place: stockbroker's office in New York City

Theme
Some people let their work life become too important.

Build Background

A Stockbroker's Life

Stockbrokers help people buy and sell stocks, or parts of a company. When a company needs money, it sells stocks. The people who buy stocks are buying a part of the company. The company gets the money it needs. The people get a sheet of paper showing that they now own a part of the company. Stockbrokers do not use ticker tape machines anymore. Instead, they use telephones and computers.

Successful stockbrokers often make a lot of money. But working as a stockbroker can be very stressful. Do you think you would you like to be a stockbroker? Why or why not?

Key Words

Read these sentences. Try to understand each word in dark type by looking at the other words in the sentence. Use a dictionary to check your ideas. Write each word and its meaning in your notebook.

1. Harvey Maxwell was a **broker** who was always busy buying and selling stocks.

2. A **romance** is a kind of story that is usually about love.

3. A **stockbroker** helps people buy or sell stocks.

4. This morning, Maxwell sold many **stocks,** or parts of a company.

5. Years ago, stockbrokers followed the buying and selling of stocks on a **ticker tape machine.** Today they use phones and computers.

Reading Strategy

Predict

As you read a story, you can **predict,** or guess, what will happen next. As you read, follow these steps:

- From time to time, stop reading to ask yourself, "What will happen next?"

- Look for clues in the story and the pictures.

- Think about what you already know about how people act.

- Think about your own experiences.

- Continue reading to see whether your prediction is correct.

The Romance of a Busy Broker

Adapted from the story by O. Henry

I

Pitcher had worked for many years in the office of Harvey Maxwell, the stockbroker. Pitcher was a quiet man. He didn't usually let his face show his feelings. But this morning he looked surprised—and very interested. Harvey Maxwell had arrived energetically as usual at 9:30. But this morning, the young lady who was his secretary had arrived with him. Pitcher watched them with interest. Harvey Maxwell didn't pay attention to Pitcher. He said only a quick "Good morning," and ran to his desk. He dug energetically into the mountain of letters and telegrams that waited for him. The stockbroker's day had begun.

Miss Leslie, the young lady, had been Maxwell's secretary for a year. She was beautiful, and she dressed simply. Unlike some secretaries, she never wore cheap glass jewelry. Her dress was gray and plain, but it fitted her body nicely. With it she wore a small black hat with a green-gold flower at the side. This morning her face shone with happiness. Her eyes were bright, her face a soft pink.

Pitcher, still interested, noticed that she acted differently this morning. Usually she walked straight inside to her own desk. But this morning she stayed in the outside office. She walked over near Maxwell's desk. Maxwell didn't seem to be a man anymore. He had changed into a busy New York stockbroker. He'd become a machine of many moving parts.

"Well—what is it? Is anything wrong?" Maxwell asked his secretary. He wasn't looking at her. His eyes were on his mail. Letters and telegrams lay on his desk like snow.

"It's nothing," she said softly. She moved away with a little smile. "Mr. Pitcher," she said, coming over to him, "did Mr. Maxwell ask you to hire another secretary yesterday?"

"Yes, he did," answered Pitcher. "He told me to get another one. I asked the secretarial school to send over a few this morning. But it's 9:45, and no one has come yet."

"I will do the work as usual, then," said the young lady, "until someone comes to fill the place." And she went to her desk at once. She hung up the black hat with the green-gold flower in its usual place.

Harvey Maxwell was always a busy stockbroker, but today he was even busier than usual. The ticker tape machine began to throw out tape. The desk telephone began to ring. Men crowded into the office, buying and selling, crying and yelling. Boys ran in and out with telegrams. Even Pitcher's face looked more alive. Maxwell pushed his chair against the wall. He ran energetically from ticker tape to telephone, jumping like a dancer.

In the middle of all this action and yelling, the stockbroker realized that someone new had arrived. He first saw a high mountain of golden hair under a large round hat. Then he noticed some large glass jewelry. Underneath all this was a young lady. Pitcher saw that Maxwell didn't know who she was. He came forward to explain. "Here is the lady from the secretarial school," Pitcher said to Maxwell. "She came for the job."

Maxwell turned around with his hands full of papers and ticker tape. "What job?" he yelled. His face looked angry.

"The secretarial job," Pitcher said quietly. "You told me yesterday to call the school. I asked them to send one over this morning."

"You're losing your mind, Pitcher! Why would I tell you a thing like that? Miss Leslie has worked well for a whole year here. The job is hers while she wants to stay. There is no job here, Madam! Tell the secretarial school, Pitcher. Don't bring any more of them in here!"

The lady turned to leave. Her hat almost hit Pitcher in the eye as she angrily walked past him out of the office. Pitcher thought to himself that Maxwell was getting more forgetful every day.

II

The office became busier and busier. Orders to buy and sell came and went like birds flying. Maxwell was worried about his own stocks, too, and worked faster and harder. This was the stock market, the world of money. There was no room in it for the world of human feelings or the world of nature.

Near lunchtime, everything quieted down. Maxwell stood by his desk with his hands full of telegrams. His pen was behind his ear. His hair stood up on his head. Suddenly through the open window came a smell of flowers, like the thin breath of spring. Maxwell stood still. This was Miss Leslie's smell, her own and only hers. The smell seemed to bring her before him. The world of the stock market disappeared. And Miss Leslie was in the next room—only twenty steps away.

"I'll do it now," said Maxwell softly. "I'll ask her now. Why didn't I do it long ago?"

He ran into her office. He jumped toward her desk. She looked up at him with a smile. Her face turned a soft pink. Her eyes were kind. Maxwell put his hands on her desk. They were still full of papers.

"Miss Leslie," he said, hurrying, "I only have a moment to talk. I want to say something important in that moment: Will you be my wife? I haven't had time to show you, but I really do love you. Speak quickly please—there's the telephone."

"Why—what are you talking about?" cried the young lady. She stood up and looked at him strangely.

"Don't you understand?" Maxwell asked quickly, looking back at the phone on his desk. "I want you to marry me. I've stolen this moment to ask you, now, while things have quieted down a little. Take the telephone, Pitcher!" he yelled. "Will you, Miss Leslie?" he added softly.

The secretary acted very strange. At first she seemed surprised. Then she began to cry. But then she smiled through her tears like the sun through rain. She put her arm around the stockbroker's neck.

"I know now," she said. "It's this business that put it out of your head. I was afraid, at first. But don't you remember, Harvey? We were married last evening at 8:00, in the little church around the corner."

Word Study

The **noun** form of some words is the same as the present tense **verb** form. For example, *surprise* is both a noun and a verb. The past tense form of such a regular verb (*surprised*) is also the **adjective** form.

Write the sentences below in your notebook. Complete each sentence with the correct form of the word. Use the chart to help you. The first item has been done for you.

Noun	Verb	Adjective
surprise	surprise	surprised
interest	interest	interested
crowd	crowd	crowded
dress	dress	dressed

1. Harvey Maxwell did not usually _____*surprise*_____ Pitcher.
   surprise/surprised

2. But Pitcher looked _____ this morning.
   surprise/surprised

3. Pitcher was _____ in the young lady's actions.
   interest/interested

4. He watched Miss Leslie with _____.
   interest/interested

5. The office was _____ with men buying and selling.
   crowd/crowded

6. This kind of _____ came into the office every day.
   crowd/crowded

7. Miss Leslie's _____ was gray.
   dress/dressed

8. The other woman was _____ in bright colors.
   dress/dressed

Extension Activity

Word Problems

The stock market is the business of buying and selling stocks. People invest their money in the stock market with the hopes of earning more money.

A. Read this sample word problem and its answer.

> Mr. Holt read about a company that made a new kind of radio. He was very excited and decided that he wanted to own stock in the company. The company was selling stocks at $3 per share. Mr. Holt bought 100 shares for which he paid $300. A few months later, the stock was selling at $5 a share. Mr. Holt's stock was now worth $500. If Mr. Holt sells the stock now, how much money will he make?

Here is the answer to the problem:

Bought 100 shares at $3 a share = $300

Now 100 shares at $5 a share = $500

$500 − $300 = $200

Money Mr. Holt will make = $200

B. Read each of the word problems. Write the answers in your notebook. Show how you arrived at your answers.

1. Lilly bought 100 shares of stock at $6 per share. She paid $600. The stock went up to $7 a share. Lilly sold the stock. How much money did she make?

2. Paul bought 50 shares of stock. Each share was $10. He paid $500. The stock went up to $12 a share. Paul sold the stock. How much money did he make?

3. Frank bought 20 shares of stock. Each share was $100. The stock fell to $50 a share. How much money will Frank lose if he sells the stock now?

Writing Practice

Write a Summary

A **summary** is a short review of the important information in a story. When you write a summary, you retell the most important ideas. A summary is much shorter than the story.

Read this summary of Part I of "The Romance of a Busy Broker."

> Pitcher worked for Harvey Maxwell, a stockbroker. One morning Pitcher thought something unusual was going on. Maxwell and his secretary, Miss Leslie, arrived at work together. The day before, Maxwell had asked Pitcher to hire a new secretary. When the new secretary arrived, Maxwell had no idea why she was there and sent her away.

Write a summary of Part II of "The Romance of a Busy Broker." Include the parts of the story you think are the most important. You might want to include the following ideas in your sentences:

- How the office got busier and busier
- What happened near lunchtime
- What Maxwell asked Miss Leslie
- Why Miss Leslie was surprised
- The surprise ending

The Ingrate

Adapted from the story by Paul Laurence Dunbar

— principle: nguyên tắc.
— endless: vô tận.
— hunger: ham muốn / khát vọng.
— advice: tư vấn
— cheating: gian lận
— honest: trung thực
— duty: nhiệm vụ / chức vụ.
— goodness: sự tốt lành
— extra: thêm.

... a man of high principle. He had often said this to Mrs. Leckler. She was often called on to listen to him. Mr. Leckler was one of those people with an endless hunger for advice, though he never acted on it. Mrs. Leckler knew this, but like a good little wife, she always offered him her little gifts of advice. Today, her husband's mind was troubled—as usual. Troubled about a question of principle.

"Mrs. Leckler," he said, "I am troubled in my mind. I'm troubled by a question of principle."

"Yes, Mr. Leckler?" his wife asked.

"If I were a cheating northern Yankee, I would be rich now. But I am too honest and generous. I always let my principles get between me and my duty." Mr. Leckler was sure of his own goodness. "Now, here is the question that troubles my principles. My slave, Josh, has been working for Mr. Eckley in Lexington. I think that city cheat has been dishonest. He lied about how many hours Josh worked, and cut down his pay for it. Now, of course, I don't care, the question of a dollar or two is nothing to *me*. But it's a different question for poor Josh." Mr. Leckler's voice became sadder. "You know, Josh wants to buy his freedom from me. And I generously give him part of what he earns. Every dollar Mr. Eckley cheats him of cuts down his pay and puts farther away his hopes of freedom."

Mrs. Leckler knew that Mr. Leckler let Josh keep only one-tenth of what he earned for extra work. So Mr. Eckley's dishonesty hurt her husband more than it hurt Josh. But she didn't say anything about that. She only asked, "But what troubles you about duty and principle here, Mr. Leckler?"

... new how to read and write

"Mr. Leckler, an you ..."

"Listen to me, my dear, and give me your advice. This is an important question. If Josh knew these things, he wouldn't be cheated when he worked away from me."

"But teaching a slave..."

"Yes, Mrs. Leckler, that's what frightens me. I know my duty—I know what the law and other people say about teaching a slave. But it is against my principles that that poor black man is being cheated. Really, Mrs. Leckler, I think I may teach him secretly, so he can defend himself."

"Well, of course," said Mrs. Leckler, "do what you think is best."

"I knew you would agree with me," he answered. "I'm glad to have your advice, my dear." And so this master of principle walked out to see his valuable slave. He was very pleased with his generosity. "I'll get Eckley next time!" he said to himself.

Josh, the subject of Mr. Leckler's principles, worked as a plasterer on Mr. Leckler's plantation, working on the walls and ceilings of the plantation's many buildings. Josh was very good at his work, and other men wanted him to work for them, too. So Mr. Leckler made money by letting Josh work on their plantations in his free time. Josh was a man of high intelligence. When he asked Mr. Leckler if he could buy his freedom with the money he made on other plantations, Mr. Leckler quickly agreed. He knew he could let his valuable slave keep only a little of the money he earned. Most of what Josh earned would belong to his master. Of course, Mr. Leckler knew that when the black man learned his numbers things would change. But it would be years before Josh could earn $2,000, the price Mr. Leckler asked for Josh's freedom. And, Mr. Leckler thought, by the time Josh came close to earning the money, the cost of a slave's freedom might suddenly go higher.

When Josh heard his master's plan, his eyes shone with pleasure, and he worked even harder than before. Even Mr. Leckler, who knew his pla[n] ... surprised how quickly Josh was learnin[g] ... figure. Mr. Leckler didn't know that on one of ... a freed slave had given Josh some lessons. Josh al[so] ... feelings of how to read before he began his lesson[s] ... certainly wasn't going to tell Mr. Leckle[r] ...

So ... passed away, and Mr. Leckler thought Josh had learned enoug[h].

"You know, Josh," he said, "I have already gone against my princ[iples] and broken the law for you. A man can't go against his principles too far, even for someone who is being cheated. I think you can take care of yourself now."

"Oh, yes, sir, I guess I can," said Josh.

"And you shouldn't be seen with any books, now."

"Oh, no, sir, certainly not," Josh said obediently. He certainly didn't plan to be seen with any books.

Just now, Mr. Leckler saw the good in what he had done. His heart was full of a great joy. Mr. Eckley was building on to his house, and asked Josh to do the plastering. When the job was done, Josh figured that Eckley had cheated him again. Eckley was very surprised when the black man looked at the numbers and showed him his dishonesty, but he passed him the two dollars. "Leckler did this," Mr. Eckley thought to himself. "Teaching a black his numbers! Leckler just wanted more money for himself! I should call the law!"

Mr. Leckler was very pleased when he heard that Josh had caught Eckley cheating. He said to himself, "Ha! I caught him, the old thief!" But to Mrs. Leckler he said, "You see, my dear, my craziness in teaching Josh was right. See how much money he saved for himself."

"What did he save?" asked the little wife without thinking.

Her husband turned red, and then answered, "Well, of course it was only 20 cents saved for *him*, but to a slave buying his freedom, every cent counts. It is not the money, Mrs. Leckler, it's the principle of the thing."

"Yes," said the lady obediently.

II

It is easy enough for the master to order the body of a slave, "This far you may go, and no further." The master has laws and chains to hold the slave back. But what master can say to the mind of a slave, "I order you to stop learning"? Josh had begun to eat the forbidden fruit of learning, and he was hungry for more. Night after night he sat by his lonely fire and read one of his few books. Other slaves laughed at him. They told him to get a wife. But Josh had no time for love or marriage. He had hopes other than to have his children be slaves to Mr. Leckler. To him, slavery was the dark night in which he dreamed of freedom. His dream was to own himself—to

- further thêm
- mind tâm trí
- learning thức học tập
- forbidden cấm
- chains: dây xích

be — master of his own body. When he thought of this, something
wo— ... his breath came hard. But he was quiet
and — ... his master, and Mr. Leckler was pleased. Usually
int— ... trouble. But who seemed more
unt— ... and to his wife, "You see, my dear,
it's — ... lack."

... North seemed to call
to Jo— ... rth he would be a
slave — ... in his freedom.
Wors— ... ll between slavery
and J— ... Then one day, when he was working away from
home, a voice called to him from the woods, "Be brave!" And later
that night the voice called to him like the north wind, "Follow."

"It seems to me that Josh should have come home tonight," said
Mr. Leckler. "But maybe he got through too late to catch a train." In
the morning he said, "Well, he's not here yet. He must have to do
some extra work. If he doesn't get home tonight, I'll go up there."

That night he did take the train to where Josh had been working.
He learned that Josh had left the night before. But where could he
have gone? For the first time, Mr. Leckler realized that Josh had run
away. Mr. Leckler was very angry. He knew that the most valuable
slave on his plantation was going north to freedom. He walked the
floor all night, but he couldn't go after Josh until morning.

Early the next day, he put the dogs on Josh's trail. The dogs
followed it into the woods, but in a few minutes they came back,
crying and lost. Josh had played an old slave trick—he had put hot
pepper in his footprints. Finally the dogs found Josh's trail further in
the woods. Leckler followed the trail until he came to a train station
about six miles away. Mr. Leckler asked the stationmaster if he had
seen a black get on the train.

"Yes," the man said, "two nights ago."

"But why did you let him go without a pass?" cried Mr. Leckler.

"I didn't," said the stationmaster. "He had a written pass signed
'James Leckler.'"

"Lies, lies!" cried Mr. Leckler. "He wrote it himself!"

"Well, how could I know?" answered the stationmaster. "Our blacks around here don't know how to write."

Mr. Leckler suddenly decided to keep quiet. Josh was probably in the arms of some Yankee abolitionist by now. There was nothing to do but put up advertisements for Josh's return. He went home and spoke angrily to his wife.

"You see, Mrs. Leckler, this is what comes of my generous heart. I taught a black to read and write. Now look how he uses this knowledge. Oh, the ingrate, the ingrate! He turns against me the weapon I gave him to defend himself! Here's the most valuable slave on my plantation gone—gone, I tell you—and all because of my kindness. It isn't his *value* I'm thinking about. It's the *principle* of the thing—the ingratitude he has shown me. Oh, if I ever catch him—!"

Just at this time, Josh was six miles north of the Ohio River. A kind Quaker was saying softly to Josh, "Lie quiet. You will be safe

he...me...him. I'll talk to him and see...your brothers or sisters wh...k has...been taken back to slavery."

Then the kind man spoke to the slave-catcher. "Oh, good evening, my friend." Josh could hear the two men talking as he hid in a bag among other bags of corn and potatoes.

It was after ten o'clock one night while Josh's bag was thrown into a wagon and driven on to the next helping hands. And in this way, hiding by day and traveling by night, Josh went north. He was helped all along the way by a few of his own people who had been freed, and always by the good Quakers. And so he made his way to Canada. And on one never-to-be-forgotten morning he stood up straight, breathed God's air, and knew himself free!

III

To Joshua Beckley, as now he was called, this life in Canada was all new and strange. It was a new thing for him to feel that he was a man among the other men he met among the whites. It was new, too, to be paid for his labor honestly. He worked more happily than he had ever done. He was even pleased at how tired his work made him feel.

Sometimes there came to his ears the stories of his brothers and sisters in the South. Other fugitive escaped slaves like himself. Their stories made him want to do something to help people he had known, escaped slaves, and the newspapers he read told him other things, too. They said that the idea of freedom was rising in the United States. Already, people were speaking out about abolishing slavery and freeing the slaves. Already people were helping those abolitionist leaders like Sumner, Phillips, Douglass, Garrison. Joshua heard the names Lucretia Mott and Harriet Beecher Stowe. And Joshua was hopeful, for after the long night of slavery he saw the first light of morning.

So the years passed. Then from those dark clouds of slavery the storm of war broke: the thunder of guns and the rain of bullets. From his home in the North Joshua watched the storm. Sometimes the war went well for the North, sometimes for the South. Then suddenly out from the storm came a cry like the voice of God, "You and your brothers and sisters are free!" Free, free, with freedom for all—not just for a few. Freedom for all who had been enslaved. Not free by escaping in the night—free to live in the light of morning.

When the northern army first called for black soldiers, Joshua went to Boston to sign up. Since he could read and write, and because of his general intelligence, he was soon made an officer. One day Mr. Leckler saw a list of names of these black soldiers. His eyes stopped at the name "Joshua Leckler." He showed the list to Mrs. Leckler.

"Mrs. Leckler," he said, "look what happened because I taught a black to read and write. I disobeyed the law of my state. I lost my slave. And I gave the Yankees a smart officer to help them fight the war. I was wrong—I was wrong. But I am right, too, Mrs. Leckler. This all happened because of my generous heart, and your bad advice. But oh, that ingrate, that ingrate!"

-enslaved : kº nõ lệ .
- army   quân đội , đám đông
- general : phổ biến , chung
- state   : tình trạng / nhà nước
- smart   : Thanh nhã , lịch sự
- advice : lời khuyên .

After You Read

Understand the Story

Answer these questions in your notebook. Write complete sentences.

1. What kind of work did Josh do on Mr. Leckler's plantation?

2. How much of what Josh earned for work on other plantations did Mr. Leckler let him keep?

3. Why was Josh trying to save money?

4. How did Josh escape, and where did he go?

5. Why did Josh put hot pepper in his footprints?

6. What did Josh become in the northern army? How did Mr. Leckler find out what Josh had done?

Elements of Literature

Characterization

Read this passage from the story. Then answer the questions.

> To Joshua Leckler, as now he was called, this life in Canada was all new and strange. It was a new thing for him to feel that he was a man like any other man he met among the whites. It was new, too, to be paid what his work was worth. He worked more happily than he had ever done. He was even pleased at how tired his work made him feel.

This passage tells how Josh has changed since the beginning of the story. Why is Josh now called "Joshua"? What other details help you understand that Josh has become a new man?

[handwritten margin notes:]
1/ Begin a new life in Canada
+ He 's officer in the northern army
- He can earn money
- He now feels equal to white people.
- He can read, study, write
- He can do mathematics → go up to higher level.
Freedom
no depent on nobrebec
Can vote.

32

Discussion

[handwritten: Two principles that describe Mr. Leckler 1- Greedy 2 - Self - interest]

Answer the questions in pairs or small groups.

1. Mr. Leckler talks a lot about his principles. He says that it is against his principles to allow a slave to be cheated. He tells Josh that he has gone against his principles in teaching him to read and do numbers. What principles is Mr. Leckler talking about? What "principles" actually control his behavior?

   [handwritten: No cheat slave]
   [handwritten: No teach black person]

2. What are some principles that you believe in strongly?

   [handwritten: everyone can cook]

Vocabulary

Choose the correct word. Write the completed sentences in your notebook.

1. Josh worked as a plasterer on Mr. Leckler's _____.
   a. slave   **b.** principles   **c.** plantation

2. Mr. Leckler said that cheating a black man went against his _____.
   a. ingrates   **b.** principles   **c.** plantations

3. A freed _____ had given Josh some reading lessons.
   a. slave   **b.** abolitionist   **c.** principle

4. Mr. Leckler called Josh _____.
   a. a Quaker   **b.** an ingrate   **c.** an abolitionist

5. _____ were people who wanted to end slavery.
   a. Ingrates   **b.** Plantations   **c.** Abolitionists

Word Study

Sometimes words have the same noun and verb forms. Usually, however, the noun form of a word is different from its verb form.

Write the sentences below in your notebook. Complete each sentence with the correct form of the word. Use the chart to help you. The first item has been done for you.

Noun	Verb
advice	advises
earnings	earns
teaching	teaches
building	builds

1. Mrs. Leckler always _____*advises*_____ Mr. Leckler.
   advice/advises

2. But he never acts on the _____ she gives him.
   advice/advises

3. Mr. Leckler lets Josh keep some of what he _____.
   earnings/earns

4. Josh's _____ are too little to buy his freedom.
   earnings/earns

5. Mr. Leckler _____ Josh to read and do numbers.
   teaching/teaches

6. Mr. Leckler's neighbors think that trouble will come
   of such _____.
   teaching/teaches

7. Mr. Eckley _____ a new room onto his house.
   building/builds

8. He hires Josh to plaster the walls of the new _____.
   building/builds

Extension Activity

Learn about Abolitionists

As you read in "The Ingrate," Joshua Leckler knew about the abolitionist leaders of the time.

A. Read about the abolitionists.

Abolitionists were people who wanted to end slavery in the United States. Abolitionists were active even in the country's earliest days. By the time of the Civil War in 1861, most abolitionists sided with the North against the South. They encouraged people to come together and speak out against slavery. They gave speeches and wrote articles for newspapers.

B. Work with a partner. Research one the following abolitionists. Take notes as you read. Prepare a brief talk to give to the class. Tell your classmates the most important facts about the person's life and work.

- Frederick Douglass
- William Lloyd Garrison
- Lucretia Mott
- Wendell Phillips
- Harriet Beecher Stowe
- Charles Sumner

Writing Practice

Write a Speech

A **speech** is a talk given before an audience. People usually write down what they want to say beforehand. Then they practice reading their speech aloud.

Read this short speech that Josh might have given at the beginning of the Civil War.

Ladies and Gentlemen, Brothers and Sisters:

My name is Joshua, and I have escaped from slavery. My former master, Mr. Leckler, let me work for other people. He kept one-tenth of the money I made. Mr. Leckler did not want to be cheated by the other people I worked for. So he taught me how to read and do numbers. My education helped me to escape. Now I am free, and the money I earn is mine. I will do all I can to help other slaves become free.

Write a speech about yourself. Tell your audience about people and places that are important to you. Talk about your favorite things to do in your free time. Help the audience get to know you better.

Before you write your speech, think about the following:

- Write an opening sentence that will get the listener's attention.

- Include details that entertain and inform your listeners.

- Try to be as natural as possible. If you don't sound real, your audience will lose interest.

A Jury of Her Peers

Adapted from the story by Susan Glaspell

> Jury. ban bồi thẩm / gian khảo.
> Peers. đồng nghiệp
> fiction. viễn tưởng.
> value giá trị.
> trapped bị mắc kẹt

About the Author

Susan Glaspell was born in 1882, in Davenport, Iowa.
She worked for a newspaper there until she earned
enough to support herself by writing fiction. She wrote
novels, short stories, and plays. In 1915, she and her
husband founded the Provincetown Playhouse in
Provincetown, Massachusetts. Glaspell first wrote "A
Jury of Her Peers" as a play called *Trifles*. The word
trifles means "small things of little value." Later, she
rewrote the play as a story. Glaspell often wrote about
people trapped by the choices they make in life. She
died in 1948.

Before [We Read]

About ["...Peers"]

Characters
Mart... ...Peters; Mrs.
Peter... ...ty attorney;
Mrs. ...

Plot
Mart... ...the wife of ... Mrs. Wright is in jail, a... husband. The sheriff needs to find a motiv... ...ing. The sheriff... ...e and Mrs. Hale find an important clue in Mrs. Wright's house. But what will they do with it?

Setting
Time: early 1900s
Place: the home of Mrs. Wright, in a farming community

Theme
People are judged most fairly by their peers.

Handwritten notes (Vietnamese glossary):
- sheriff — cảnh sát
- attorney — luật sư
- scene — cảnh / bối cảnh
- crime — tội phạm
- jail — nhà tù
- accused — bị buộc tội
- motive — động cơ
- judged — đánh giá
- fairly — khá / công bằng / tốt
- peers — đồng nghiệp
- trial — thử nghiệm / sự án
- based — dựa trên
- facts — sự kiện
- serve — phục vụ
- cases — trường hợp
- jurors — hội thẩm

Build Background

A Jury
A jury is a group of people at a trial who decide if a person is guilty of a crime. A jury can have six to twelve members. Jury members make their decisions based on the facts that are presented to them during the trial. At the time this story was written, women were not allowed to serve on a jury. That meant that women's cases were decided by male jurors.

Do you think male jurors would be able to decide a woman's case fairly? Why or why not?

Mrs. Wright
Martha Hale
Mr. Hale
Peters
Mrs. Peters
Mr. Henderson
Susan Glaspell

Key Words

Read these sentences. [obscured]
by looking at the other [obscured]
check your ideas. Write [obscured]
notebook.

1. The woman needed [obscured]
   in court.

2. The police will look f[obscured]
   committed the crime[obscured]

3. No one could figure out the woman's **motive,** or reason, for doing such a terrible thing.

4. The police found a **rope** tied around the dead person's neck.

5. The local **sheriff,** or policeman, went to the house where the body was found.

attorney
clues
motive
rope
sheriff

Reading Strategy

Skim a Text

When you **skim a text,** you read it quickly to get a general idea of what it is about. To skim this story, follow these steps:

- Read the first and second paragraphs quickly.
- Read only the first sentences of the following paragraphs.
- Read the last paragraph quickly.

Then answer the following questions:

1. Where does the story take place?

2. Who are the main characters?

3. What kind of story is it? Is it funny? Serious? Scary?

...king, half the flour sifted and half unsifted. She hated to see things half done. But it was no ordinary thing that called her away. It was probably further from ordinary than anything that had ever happened in Dickson County.

She had been sifting flour when the sheriff drove up with his horse and buggy to get Mr. Hale. Sheriff Peters had asked Mrs. Hale to come, too. His wife was nervous, he said with a grin. She wanted another woman to come along. So Martha Hale had dropped everything right where it was.

"Martha!" her husband's voice came, "don't keep the folks waiting out here in the cold!"

She tied the wool shawl tighter and climbed into the buggy. Three men and a woman were waiting for her. Martha Hale had met Mrs. Peters, the sheriff's wife, at the county fair. Mrs. Peters didn't seem like a sheriff's wife. She was small and thin and ordinary. She didn't have a strong voice. But Mr. Peters certainly did look like a sheriff. He was a heavy man with a big voice, very friendly to folks who followed the law. But now, Mrs. Hale thought, he was going to the Wrights' house as a sheriff, not a friend.

The Wrights' house looked lonely this cold March morning. It had always been a lonely looking house. It was down in a valley, and the poplar trees around it were lonely looking trees. The men were talking about what had happened there: her husband, Sheriff Peters,

and the county attorney, Mr. Hend[...]
Peters.

"I'm glad you came with me," M[...]

When the buggy reached the d[...]
could not go inside. She had often s[...]
and see Minnie Foster." She still th[...]
though for twenty years she had [...]
always something to do, and Min[...]
mind. She felt sad that she had c[...]

The men went over to stand [...]
together by the door. At first, they didn't e[...]
kitchen.

"Now, Mr. Hale," the sheriff began. "Before we move things
around, you tell Mr. Henderson what you saw when you came here
yesterday morning."

II

Mrs. Hale felt nervous for her husband. Lewis Hale often lost his
way in a story. She hoped he would tell it straight this time.
Unnecessary things would just make it harder for Minnie Foster.

"Yes, Mr. Hale?" the county attorney said.

"I started to town with a load of potatoes," Mrs. Hale's husband
began. "I came along this road, and I saw the house. I said to myself,
'I'm going to see John Wright about the telephone.' They will bring a
telephone out here if I can get somebody else to help pay for it. I'd
spoken to Wright before, but he said folks talked too much already.
All *he* asked for was peace and quiet. I guess you know how much he
talked himself. But I thought I would ask him in front of his wife. All
the women like the telephone. In this lonely road it would be a good
thing. Not that he cared much about what his wife wanted . . ."

Now there he was!—saying things he didn't need to say. Mrs.
Hale tried to catch her husband's eye, but luckily the attorney
interrupted him with:

"Just tell what happened when you got there, Mr. Hale."

Mr. Hale began his story. "I knocked at the door. But it was all quiet inside. I knew they must be up—it was past eight o'clock. I knocked again, and I thought I heard someone say, 'Come in.' I opened the door"—Mr. Hale pointed toward the door where he had entered—"And there, in that rocking chair"—he pointed to it—"sat Mrs. Wright."

"How did she—look?" the county attorney asked.

"Well," said Hale, "she looked—strange."

"How do you mean—strange?"

The attorney took out a notebook and pencil. Mrs. Hale did not like that pencil. She kept her eye on her husband, as if to tell him, "No unnecessary things. They'll just go into that notebook and make trouble." Hale spoke carefully, as if the pencil made him think more slowly.

"Well, she didn't seem to know what she was going to do next. I said, 'How do, Mrs. Wright. It's cold isn't it?' And she said, 'Is it?' and sat there fingering her apron, nervouslike.

"Well, I was surprised. She didn't ask me to come in and sit down, but just sat there, not even looking at me. And so I said, 'I want to see John.'

"And then she—laughed. I guess you'd call it a laugh.

"I said, a little sharp, 'Can I see John?'

"'No,' she said, kind of dull. 'Isn't he home?' said I. 'Yes,' says she, 'he's home.' 'Then why can't I see him?' I asked her. Now I was angry. 'Because he's dead,' says she—all quiet and dull. She fingered her apron some more.

"'Why, where is he?' I said, not knowing *what* to say.

"She just pointed upstairs—like this," said Hale, pointing. "Then I said, 'Why, what did he die of?'

"'He died of a rope around his neck,' says she, and just went on fingering her apron."

Nobody spoke. Everyone looked at the rocking chair as if they saw the woman who had sat there yesterday.

"And w[...] at last interrupted the silence.

"I wen[...] —lying on the— he was dea[...] ought I'd better not touch[...] anything. So I went dow[...]

"'Who [...] I ask sharp, and she stops fingering h[...] I know,' she says. 'You don't know?' said I. 'Weren't y[...] same bed with him. Somebody tied a rope arour[...] killed him, and you didn't wake up?'

"'I did[...] she says after me[...]

"I may have looked as if I didn't see how that could be. After a minute she said, 'I sleep sound.'

"I thought maybe she ought to tell her story first to the sheriff. So I went as fast as I could to the nearest telephone—over at the Rivers' place on High Road. Then I came back here to wait for Sheriff Peters.

"I thought I should talk to her. So I said I had stopped by to see if John wanted to put in a telephone. At that, she started to laugh, and then she stopped and looked frightened. . . ."

The attorney spoke to the sheriff. "I guess we'll go upstairs first—then out to the barn and around there. You made sure yesterday that there's nothing important here in the kitchen?"

"Nothing here but kitchen things," said the sheriff with a laugh.

The attorney was searching in the cupboard. After a minute he pulled out his hand, all sticky.

"Here's a nice mess," he said angrily.

"Oh—her fruit," Mrs. Peters said. She looked at Mrs. Hale. "She was worried about her fruit when it turned cold last night. She said the stove might go out, and the jars might break."

Mrs. Peters' husband began to laugh. "Well, how about that for a woman! Held in jail for murder, and worrying about her jars of fruit!"

The attorney answered, "I guess before we finish with her, she may have something more important to worry about."

"Oh, well," Mr. Hale said, "v[...] nothing."

"And yet," said the attorney, [...] ladies?" He smiled at the wome[n ...] smile back.

The lawyer washed his hand[...]

"Dirty towels!" he said. "Not [...] He kicked some messy pans und[er ...]

"There's a lot of work to do a[...] sharply. "And men's hands aren't [...]

"Ah! You feel a duty to your s[ex, I see]" He laughed. "But you and Mrs. Wright were neighbors. I guess you were friends, too."

"I've not seen much of her these years."

"And why was that? You didn't like her?"

"I liked her well enough. Farmers' wives have their hands full, Mr. Henderson. And then—it never seemed like a very happy place . . ."

"You mean the Wrights didn't get on very well together?"

"No. I don't mean anything. But I don't think a place would be happier if John Wright was in it."

"I'd like to talk to you more about that, Mrs. Hale. But first we'll look upstairs."

The sheriff said to the attorney, "I suppose anything Mrs. Peters does will be all right? She came to take Mrs. Wright some clothes— and a few little things."

"Of course," said the attorney. "Mrs. Peters is one of us. Maybe you women may come on a clue to the motive—and that's the thing we need."

Mr. Hale smiled, ready to make a joke. "Yes, but would the women know a clue if they did come upon it?"

III

The women stood silent while the men went upstairs. Then Mrs. Hale began to clean the messy pans under the sink.

Handwritten margin notes:
- dried khô
- dishtowel món ăn (khăn)
- kicked đá
- messy lộn xộn
- pans chảo
- sink chìm
- farm trang trại
- sharply mạnh / gian lận
- duty nhiệm vụ
- wives vợ
- suppose giả sử
- clue đầu mối
- joke trò đùa

bag bao
cupboard tủ, nhất / đào
picked chọn
lively sống động
jail nhà tù
case trường hợp
anger tức giận
low thấp

"I would hate to have men coming into my kitchen, looking around and talking about my housework."

"Of course," Mrs. Peters said. But Mrs. Hale was looking around. She saw a box of sugar. Next to it was a paper bag half full.

"She was putting this in there," she said to herself. Work begun and not finished. She saw the table—a dish towel lay on it. One half of the table was clean. What had interrupted Minnie Foster?

"I must get her things from the cupboard," Mrs. Peters said. "Are you coming with me, Mrs. Hale?" she asked nervously.

Together they found the few clothes Mrs. Wright had asked for. Mrs. Hale picked up an old black skirt.

"My, John Wright hated to spend money!" she said. "She used to be lively. She used to wear pretty clothes and sing in the church, when she was Minnie Foster . . ." Martha Hale looked at Mrs. Peters and thought: she doesn't care that Minnie Foster had pretty clothes when she was a girl.

But then she looked at Mrs. Peters again, and she wasn't so sure. In fact, she had never been sure about Mrs. Peters. She seemed so nervous, and yet her eyes looked as if they could see a long way into things.

"Is this all you want to take to the jail?" Martha Hale asked.

"No, she wanted an apron and her woolen shawl." Mrs. Peters took them from the cupboard.

"Mrs. Peters!" cried Mrs. Hale suddenly. "Do you think she did it?"

Mrs. Peters looked frightened. "Oh, I don't know," she said.

"Well, I don't think she did," Mrs. Hale said. "Asking for her apron and her shawl. Worrying about her fruit."

"Mr. Peters says it looks bad for her," Mrs. Peters answered. "Saying she didn't wake up when someone tied that rope around his neck. Mr. Henderson said that what this case needs is a motive. Something to show anger—or sudden feeling."

"Well, I think it's kind of low to lock her up in jail, and then come out here to look for clues in her own house," said Martha Hale.

"But, Mrs. Hale," said the sheriff's wife, "

Mrs. Hale turned to re-light the stove. "I
cook on this broken thing year after year—

Mrs. Peters looked from the broken stov
on the sink. Water had to be carried in from
person gets so *down*—and loses heart."

And again Mrs. Peters' eyes had that loo
seeing through things.

"Oh, look, Mrs. Hale. She was sewing a
up a sewing basket full of quilt blocks.

The women were studying the quilt as the men came downstairs. Just as the door opened, Mrs. Hale was saying, "Do you think she was going to quilt it, or just knot it?"

"Quilt it or knot it!" laughed the sheriff. "They're worrying about a quilt!" The men went out to look in the barn.

"I don't see what is so funny," said Mrs. Hale.

Then Mrs. Peters said in a strange voice, "Why, look at this one." She held up a quilt block. "The sewing. All the rest were sewed so nice. But this one is so *messy*—"

Mrs. Hale took the quilt block. She pulled out the sewing and started to replace bad sewing with good.

"Oh, I don't think we ought to touch anything . . ." Mrs. Peters said helplessly.

"I'll just finish this end," said Mrs. Hale, quietly.

"Mrs. Hale?"

"Yes, Mrs. Peters?"

"What do you think she was so nervous about?"

"Oh, *I* don't know. I don't know that she was—nervous. Sometimes I sew badly when I'm tired."

She looked quickly at Mrs. Peters, but Mrs. Peters was looking far away. Later she said in an ordinary voice, "Here's a birdcage. Did she have a bird, Mrs. Hale? It seems kind of funny to think of a bird here. I wonder what happened to it."

"Oh, probably the cat got it."

"But look, the door has been broken. It [...] rough with it."

Their eyes met, worrying and wonderin[...]

"I'm glad you came with me, Mrs. Hale[...] me—sitting here alone."

"I wish I had come over here sometime[...] answered Mrs. Hale. "I stayed away because[...] Did you know John Wright, Mrs. Peters?"

"Not really. They say he was a good ma[...]

"Well—good," Mrs. Hale said. "He didr[...] bills. But he was a hard man. His voice was like the north wind that cuts to the bone. You didn't know—her, did you, Mrs. Peters?"

"Not until they brought her to the jail yesterday."

"She was—she was like a little bird herself. . . . Why don't you take the quilt blocks in to her? It might take up her mind."

"That's a nice idea, Mrs. Hale," agreed the sheriff's wife. She took more quilt blocks and a small box out of the sewing basket.

"What a pretty box," Mrs. Hale said. "That must be something she had from a long time ago, when she was a girl." Mrs. Hale opened the box. Quickly her hand went to her nose.

Mrs. Peters bent closer. "It's the bird," she said softly. "Someone broke its neck."

Just then the men came in the door. Mrs. Hale slipped the box under the quilt blocks.

"Well, ladies," said the county attorney, "have you decided if she was going to quilt it or knot it?" He smiled at them.

"We think," began the sheriff's wife nervously, "that she was going to—knot it."

"That's interesting, I'm sure," he said, not listening. "Well, there's no sign that someone came in from the outside. And it was their own rope. Now let's go upstairs again . . ." The men left the kitchen again.

"She was going to bury the bird in that pretty box," said Mrs. Hale.

"When I was _fit_ ___ ____ softly. "my kitten—-there was a boy who murdered it, in front of my eyes. If they hadn't held me back, I would have—hurt him."

They sat without speaking or moving.

"Wright wouldn't like the bird. A thing that sang. She used to sing. He killed that, too," Mrs. Hale said slowly.

"Of course, we don't *know* who killed the bird," said Mrs. Peters.

"I knew John Wright," Mrs. Hale answered. "There had been years and years of—nothing. Then she had a bird to sing to her. It would be so—silent—when it stopped."

"I know what silence is," Mrs. Peters said in a strange voice. "When my first baby died, after two years . . ."

"Oh, I *wish* I'd come over here sometimes. *That* was a crime!" Mrs. Hale cried.

But the men were coming back. "No, Peters, it's all clear. Except the reason for doing it. If there was some real clue . . . Something to show the jury . . . You go back to town, Sheriff. I'll stay and look around some more."

Mrs. Hale looked at Mrs. Peters. Mrs. Peters was looking at her.

"Do you want to see what Mrs. Peters is bringing to the jail?" the sheriff asked the attorney.

"Oh, I guess the ladies haven't picked up anything very dangerous," he answered. "After all, a sheriff's wife is married to the law. Did you ever think of your duty that way, Mrs. Peters?"

"Not—just that way," said Mrs. Peters quietly.

The men went out to get the buggy, and the women were alone for one last moment.

Mrs. Hale pointed to the sewing basket. In it was the thing that would keep another woman in jail.

For a moment Mrs. Peters did not move. Then she ran to get the box. She tried to put it in her little handbag, but it didn't fit.

There was the sound of the door opening. Martha Hale took the box and put it quickly in her big pocket.

"Well, Peters," said the county attorney jokingly, "at least we found out that she was not going to quilt it. She was going to—what do you call it, ladies?"

Mrs. Hale put her hand against her pocket. "We call it—knot it, Mr. Henderson."

After You Read

Understand the Story

Answer these questions in your notebook. Write complete sentences.

1. What was Mrs. Hale doing when the sheriff arrived? Why did the sheriff want her to come with the others?

2. What did Mr. Hale find when he stopped by the Wrights' house?

3. What did the attorney need to find for the jury?

4. What did the women notice about one of Mrs. Wright's quilt blocks? What did Mrs. Hale do with it?

5. What was in the box the women found in the sewing basket?

6. What did Mrs. Hale do with the box? Why?

Elements of Literature

Theme

Read this passage from the story. Then answer the questions.

> "Oh, well," Mr. Hale said, "women are used to worrying about nothing."
>
> "And yet," said the attorney, "what would we do without the ladies?" He smiled at the women, but they did not speak, did not smile back.

The theme of the story is that people are judged most fairly by their peers. How do the male characters in the passage above show that they have little respect for the ladies in the story? Do you think that they would have understood Mrs. Wright's motive for killing her husband? Why or why not?

1900, men control women

Discussion

Answer the questions in pairs or small groups.

1. What clues lead Mrs. Hale and Mrs. Peters to believe that Mrs. Wright killed her husband? Do these clues prove that Mrs. Wright killed her husband? Explain.

2. Is it wrong of Mrs. Hale and Mrs. Peters not to give the clues they find to the sheriff? Why or why not?

3. Mrs. Hale and Mrs. Peters are Mrs. Wright's peers. In what way do they also become her jury?

Vocabulary

Choose the correct word. Write the completed sentences in your notebook.

1. Mr. Peters was the _____ of Dickson County.
   a. sheriff   **b.** doctor   **c.** attorney

2. Mr. Henderson was the county _____.
   a. sheriff   **b.** farmer   **c.** attorney

3. Somebody tied a _____ around Mr. Wright's neck.
   a. clue   **b.** rope   **c.** motive

4. Mr. Henderson needed to find a _____ for the killing.
   a. rope   **b.** quilt   **c.** motive

5. Mrs. Hale and Mrs. Peters found _____ to the murder.
   a. clues   **b.** ropes   **c.** fruit jars

Word Study

Write the sentences below in your notebook. Complete each sentence with the correct form of the word. Use the chart to help you. The first item has been done for you.

Noun	Adjective	Adverb
peace	peaceful	peacefully
nervousness	nervous	nervously
duty	dutiful	dutifully
mess	messy	messily

1. Mr. Wright liked a quiet life, but he wasn't a _____*peaceful*_____
   peace/peaceful
   man.

2. After her arrest, Mrs. Wright went _____ to jail.
   peaceful/peacefully

3. Mrs. Hale was _____ when her husband told his story.
   nervous/nervousness

4. Mrs. Peters looked away _____ from Mrs. Hale.
   nervous/nervously

5. The attorney said that Mrs. Peters was "one of us" to remind her that she had a _____ to follow the law.
   duty/dutifully

6. Was Mrs. Hale a less _____ woman than Mrs. Peters?
   duty/dutiful

7. Mrs. Wright's kitchen was _____.
   messy/messily

8. The broken fruit jars made a _____ in the cupboard.
   mess/messy

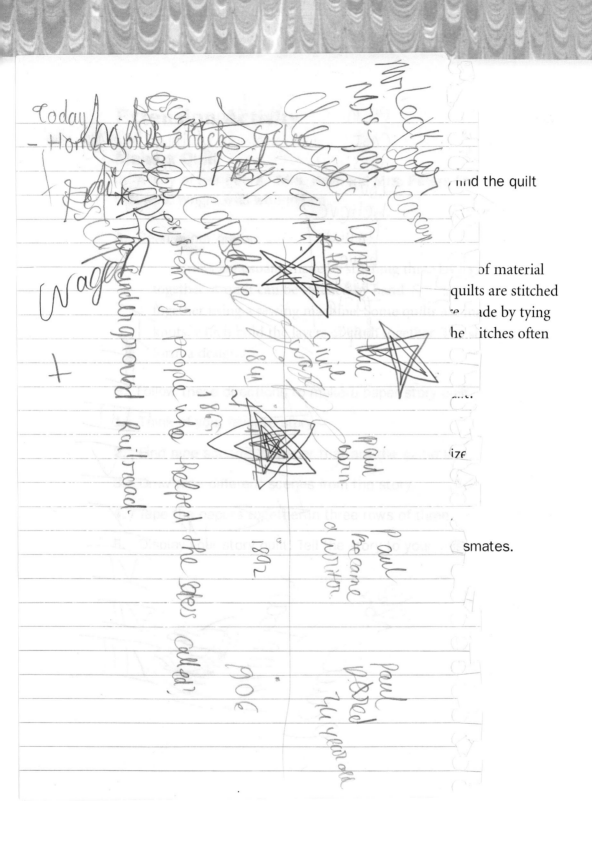

nd the quilt

of material
quilts are stitched
de by tying
he itches often

ize

smates.

Writing Practice

Write a Dialogue

Dialogue is the conversation between characters in a story. Reading what characters say helps you understand them. A writer uses quotation marks to show the exact words a character says. Here is an example:

> "How did she—look?" the county attorney asked.

Good writers use a variety of verbs when writing dialogue. Read this dialogue. It is an imaginary conversation between Mr. and Mrs. Hale.

> "Where are you going?" *asked* Mrs. Hale.
>
> "I am going to town," Mr. Hale *answered*.
>
> "When will you be back?" *said* Mrs. Hale.
>
> "I will be back at about six," Mr. Hale *replied*. "I need to see the sheriff. He is meeting me in town."
>
> "I would like to go, too," Mrs. Hale *thought* to herself.

Write a page of dialogue for a conversation between two characters in a story that you have read. Remember to use quotation marks and a variety of verbs.

The Whale Hunt

Adapted from the novel Moby Dick *by Herman Melville*

About the Author

Herman Melville was born in 1819 in New York City. In 1841, he went to sea on a whaling ship. Melville's years at sea were the subject of several novels he wrote after his return. "The Whale Hunt" is from *Moby Dick*, published in 1851. This novel tells what happens on board the *Pequod* as its crew hunts a huge whale. Today we consider *Moby Dick* one of the greatest American novels. During his last twenty-five years, Melville worked as a customs inspector. He wrote poetry during this time, but his early popularity fell away. Before his death in 1891, Melville wrote another book about life at sea, *Billy Budd*. This novel brought him fame once more.

Before You Read

About "The Whale Hunt"

Characters
Ishmael, the narrator; Queequeg, Fedallah, and Daggoo—harpooners; Tashtego, a lookout; Captain Ahab; Starbuck, Stubb, and Flask—other boat crew chiefs

Plot
Sailors on the *Pequod* are at sea hunting whales. They spot a group of whales. Four boats are lowered into the water to go after the whales. The sea is rough. The sailors are in danger in more ways than one.

Setting
Time: the 1840s
Place: the *Pequod*, a whaling ship from Nantucket, Massachusetts

Theme
The powerful forces of nature are often beyond people's control.

Build Background

Whaling Days
In the 1700s, sailors in New England hunted whales for their oil. People burned whale oil in lamps to light their homes. They also used whale oil to make soap. Life on a whaling ship was difficult. Sometimes there were huge storms. Sometimes there was no wind at all. Whale hunters, also called whalers, were away from home for months or even years.

With a partner, share what you know about whales, ships, or sailing.

Key Words

Read these sentences. Try to understand each word in dark type by looking at the other words in the sentence. Use a dictionary to check your ideas. Write each word and its meaning in your notebook.

bow

crew

harpoons

leeward

schools

sperm whale

stern

1. The man stood in the front of the ship, or the **bow.**

2. The **crew,** a group of sailors, worked on the ship.

3. Whalers used long, sharp spears called **harpoons** to kill the whale.

4. The ship sailed in a **leeward** direction—with the wind.

5. Whales swim in **schools** because swimming in a group gives the whales a sense of community as well as safety.

6. Moby Dick was a **sperm whale,** a large toothed whale that can grow to be 60 feet long.

7. A sailor at the back of the ship, the **stern,** called out to the rest of the crew.

Reading Strategy

Text Structure

Looking at the **structure** of a **text** can help you tell what kind of text you are reading. Novels and short stories, poems, and plays all look different.

- Novels and short stories are written in paragraphs. Dialogue is placed inside quotation marks.

- Poems are usually written line by line, rather than in paragraphs. Poetry doesn't always follow the same punctuation rules as other types of text.

- Plays are mainly dialogue. Each character's name is followed by a colon (:) and the words the character says. Stage directions are placed inside parentheses.

As you read "The Whale Hunt," look for the text features that tell you it is a short story rather than a poem or a play.

The Whale Hunt

Adapted from the novel Moby Dick *by Herman Melville*

I

It was a hot, still afternoon. Storm clouds were gathering overhead. The whaling ship, *Pequod,* out of Nantucket, sailed smoothly across the lead-gray sea. The seamen were lazily lying on deck, or staring from the masts out to sea. All the men were still—still, too, the gray waters. Each silent sailor turned to his own dreaming.

I, Ishmael, was one of that crew. I had signed onto the *Pequod* in Nantucket with Queequeg, a Polynesian harpooner of great strength and skill. We had become friends sailing with these men for many empty days, with no sight of a whale. We had worked with the men; we had eaten, sung, and shouted with them. Now Queequeg and I sat with the others on deck, our hands slowly working with ropes and tools, our minds lost in thought and silence.

Suddenly I heard a cry so strange, so wild, that the rope fell from my hand. I stood looking up at the dark clouds from which that voice had dropped like a wing. High up in the highest mast was our lookout, Tashtego, an Indian from Martha's Vineyard Island in Massachusetts. His body was reaching eagerly forward, his hand pointing straight ahead. His wild cry was the cry of whalemen all over the seas, from lookouts high up in the masts. But Tashtego's was the most unearthly and musical voice of all.

"There she blows! There! There! There! She blows! She blows!"

"Where-away?"

"There, to leeward, about two miles off! A school of them! Sperm whales, men!"

Instantly, everything was moving as we prepared for the hunt.

The sperm whale blows its jets of air and water as regularly as a clock ticks. This is how whalemen know them from other kinds of whale. The sperm whale is a clever, even tricky animal when it knows it is being hunted. But these whales had not seen us yet. Therefore the *Pequod* was now kept away from the wind, and she went gently rolling before it. We expected the whales to rise up in front of our bow.

The men not already on deck dropped down from the masts on ropes. The tubs that held ropes for the harpoons were set out on deck. The boat crews gathered by their boats. We swung the four boats from the deck of the *Pequod* out over the sea.

"All ready, Fedallah?" Captain Ahab cried to his harpooner, a dark, dangerous-looking man from the East Asian islands.

"Ready," was the half-hissed reply. Fedallah wore a black Chinese jacket; his white hair was wrapped round and round his head. He had the hard, silent, deadly look that ordinary people see only in fearful dreams.

"Lower the boats, then, do you hear? Lower away!" Captain Ahab shouted to the boat crew chiefs. The four boats were quickly lowered. The eager crews acted with an unconscious daring that is unknown in other professions. They jumped goat-like from the high deck of the *Pequod* down into the boats rolling on the waves below.

Captain Ahab stood tall in the stern of his boat. "Spread yourselves widely, all boats," he called to Starbuck, Stubb, and Flask, the other boat crew chiefs. "You, Flask, pull out more to leeward."

"Aye, aye, Sir," little Flask answered happily. He swung around the great oar that steered his boat. "Lay back on those oars!" he ordered his crew. "There! There! There again! There she blows right ahead, boys! Lay back!"

Starbuck was chief of my boat. Like the other crew chiefs, he stood in the stern of the boat holding the steering oar. We faced him, our backs to the whales ahead. As we headed past Stubb's boat, we could hear him talking to his crew: "Pull, pull on those oars, my fine hearts! Pull, my children, pull, my little ones," he called in a voice that was strong and low, smooth and musical. "Why don't you break your backbones, my boys? Still asleep, are you? Pull, will you? Pull, can't you? Pull, won't you? That's the way you'll get your gold, my lovely fellows! Hurrah for the gold cup of sperm oil, my heroes! Yes, and easy, easy; don't be in a hurry—don't be in a hurry. Why don't you break your oars, you dogs! That's it—that's it; long and strong. Bite on something, you devils! Here!" he said, pulling his knife from his belt, "every mother's son of you, pull out your knife, and put it between your teeth! That's it, my great hearts, my children, that's it! Now you're pulling like something! Now you are strong as that steel blade, my boys!" That is how Stubbs taught his men the religion of rowing. He would say the most terrifying things to his crew, his voice full of fun and fury. But the fury only added to the fun, and in the end they pulled at their oars for the joke of the thing.

Starbuck, too, pushed us onward toward the whales. He spoke in a low voice, almost a hissing whisper, so deep was his passion for the hunt. "Strong, boys, strong. There's tubs of sperm oil ahead, and that's what we came for! Pull, my boys—sperm oil's the game. This is our duty and our profit. Duty and profit, hand in hand—pull boys!" Duty and profit: this was Starbuck's religion.

Captain Ahab steered his boat ahead of the others. His crew of Manila seamen were as strong as steel and whalebone. In the bow of the boat stood Fedallah, his harpoon ready. In the stern, old Ahab stood ready at the steering oar, as he had done in a thousand boat-lowerings before. All at once, his arm rose into the air in an odd movement and then remained fixed. His five oarsmen stopped pulling. Boat and crew sat still on the sea. Instantly, the three other boats behind Ahab paused on their way. The whales had suddenly and smoothly lowered themselves deeper down into the blue. Only Ahab, closer to them, had seen their movement. For the moment, the huge whales had disappeared.

II

"Every man look out along his oar!" Starbuck called to us. "You, Queequeg, stand up!" Queequeg's heart and harpoon were ready.

He stood up tall in the bow, his eager eyes on the spot where the whales were last seen. Starbuck stood in the stern coolly balancing himself to the rolling boat. Silently, searchingly, he eyed the wide blue eye of the sea.

Not very far away from us, Flask's boat lay breathlessly still. Flask stood in the stern, on the narrow top of a strong, thick post used to guide the harpoon ropes when a harpooned whale pulls the boat along behind it. The post was short. Flask, too, was short—small and short. At the same time, he was big and tall in his passion. The post did not satisfy him.

"I can't see three waves off. Hold up an oar, there, and let me stand on that."

At his chief's word, Daggoo, Flask's huge African harpooner, moved to the stern. "I'm as good an oar as any, Sir," he said. "Will you climb up?"

With that, Daggoo planted his feet against the sides of the boat. He held out his hands to help Flask climb. Flask jumped up high and dry on Daggoo's shoulders.

"Thank you very much, my fine fellow," said Flask. "Only, I wish you fifty feet taller!"

At any time it is a strange sight to see the wonderfully unconscious ability of the whaleman. He can stand firmly balanced in his boat even when the seas are rolling and crashing furiously under his feet.

But to see the little Flask atop the tall Daggoo was even stranger. The black man rolled with every roll of the sea, and with the cool, easy, unthinking command of a king. And though chief of the boat, Flask balanced like a snowflake on Daggoo's broad back. Now and then, Flask would shout, or stamp his foot on Daggoo's shoulder in his eagerness to find the whales. But Daggoo never moved, except with the roll of the sea. So it is with human wishes: We shout and stamp upon the forgiving earth in our passion, but the earth does not change her seas or seasons because of us.

Meanwhile, in the third boat, Stubb showed no such far-looking passion as Starbuck and Flask. The whales might be down for a short dive out of fear, or a longer dive to find food. In either case, Stubb would wait calmly with the aid of his pipe. He pulled it out of his hatband, where he always wore it like a feather. But he hardly had time to light a match across the rough skin of his hand. Tashtego, Stubb's harpooner, stood with eyes staring to leeward like two fixed stars. Suddenly he dropped down to his seat.

"Down, down all, and pull!—There they are!" he cried.

No landsman would have sensed the nearness of the whales at that moment. Nothing showed but a troubled bit of greenish water. A thin white fog blew past the waves to leeward. The air around seemed to move, like the air over heated plates of steel. And beneath this troubled pool of air and sea the whales moved onward, faster, faster than the boats could row.

"Pull, pull, my good boys," Starbuck called to us in his low-hissed, passionate whisper. He did not say much to his crew, nor did we say much to him. But the silence of the boat was sometimes broken by his strange whispers, now sharp with command, now soft with begging.

How different from Starbuck was Flask! "Sing out and roar, my good hearts! Row our boat to the whale's broad back! On, on! Pull, pull!—only get me there, and I will give you my house, my wife, my children. Row on! I will go mad! Look at that white water!" Flask pulled his hat from his head, stamped up and down on it, picked it up, and finally threw it into the rolling sea.

"Look at that fellow now," said Stubb philosophically to his own crew. "He's all in a fury! Yes, let him be. But you, boys, pull smoothly onwards. Happily, happily—sweet pudding for supper, happy's the word. But pull softly—smooth, now—on those oars. Only pull, and keep pulling. Crack your backbones and bite your knives in two! Take it easy, I say. Take it easy, but break your heart and bones!"

But what Captain Ahab said to his crew—those words should not be written here. Only the sharks in the terrific sea should give ear to his furious words, or see his eyes full of red murder. So did Ahab race to the hunt.

III

The chase was a scene full of quick wonder. The huge waves of the all-powerful sea rolled and roared. The men would take a deep breath as their boat balanced atop a wave sharp enough to cut it in two. Then they would slide down the other side, the harpooners and crew chiefs shouting, the oarsmen struggling. Then the long hard row up the opposite hill and the terrifying slide again down its other side. And behind the boats the wonderful sight of the *Pequod* following fast, her sails wide to the wind. All this filled, and overfilled, the men's hearts. No one can feel stranger or stronger passion than one who for the first time enters the furious circle of the hunted sperm whale.

The dancing white water over the whales was becoming more visible as the clouds darkened. The jets of water and air coming from the whales began to spread out right and left as the whales separated from each other. Our boats pulled further apart, following them.

On Starbuck's boat, we had put up our sail. We rushed forward so fast in the rising wind that the leeward oars were almost torn from our hands. As the storm gathered, fog blew down over the waves. Soon we were running through a thick cloud of it and could see neither the big ship *Pequod* nor any of the other small boats.

"There's white water again, men," Starbuck whispered. "There's time yet to kill a whale before the storm breaks. Stand up, Queequeg!" Queequeg, harpoon in his hand, stood tall. "There's his back," said Starbuck. "*There, there,* give it to him!"

A short, hissing sound leapt out of the boat; it was the pointed steel of Queequeg's harpoon. Then, all in a terrific movement, an unseen push came up under the stern. The bow of the boat seemed to strike a hill. Something rolled and thundered beneath us just as

the storm broke overhead. The sail blew apart into pieces. The boat turned, and we were thrown, breathless, into the furious white waves. Storm, whale, and harpoon had all mixed together. And the whale, only touched by the steel, escaped.

The boat was half filled with water but not broken. Swimming round it, we caught the floating oars and pulled ourselves back into the boat. There we sat, up to our knees in the sea, the water covering every bone and board.

Now the wind increased to a howl, and the waves crashed around the boat and into it. Thunder and lightning roared and cracked around us. We shouted to the other boats, but our voices were lost in the noise of the wind and waves. The fog and the shadows of night hid the *Pequod* from us completely.

Starbuck struggled with the waterproof matchbox. After many failures he managed to light a tiny lamp. He handed it to Queequeg to tie to the end of his harpoon. There, then, he sat, holding up that foolish candle in the heart of that terrible emptiness. There, then, he sat, through the dark hours of the night, hopelessly holding up hope in the middle of nothingness.

Wet to the bone, cold to the heart, we lifted our eyes as morning came on in the dark sky. Fog still lay spread out over the sea. The empty lamp lay broken at the bottom of the boat. Suddenly Queequeg jumped up, holding a hand to his ear. Through the lessening sounds of the storm, we could hear a faint sighing and cracking of ropes and masts in the wind.

The sound came nearer and nearer, until the fog was broken by a huge, ghostly form. Terrified, we jumped into the sea as the *Pequod* rose up behind and above us, only a ship's length away.

Floating on the waves, we watched as our empty boat was pulled under the *Pequod*'s bow, like a wood chip in a waterfall. Then it was gone. We swam hard toward the *Pequod*. We were thrown against its side by the crashing waves, but at last were taken up and safely landed on board the ship.

And what of the other whale boats? Before the storm closed in, the other crews had cut loose from their whales and returned to the *Pequod* in good time. They all believed that our crew was lost under the furious waves. But still they sailed nearby, thinking to find a sign of our passing—a lonely oar, perhaps, floating on the endless sea.

Word Study

Write the sentences below in your notebook. Complete each sentence with the correct form of the word. Use the chart to help you. The first item has been done for you.

Noun	Adjective	Adverb
fury	furious	furiously
laziness	lazy	lazily
passion	passionate	passionately
terror	terrifying	terrifyingly

1. Ahab's murderous eyes were filled with _____ fury _____.
   fury/furious

2. Flask jumped up and down _____.
   furious/furiously

3. The men were not permitted to be _____ for long.
   lazy/lazily

4. As soon as a whale was spotted, their _____ instantly disappeared.
   lazy/laziness

5. The men were _____ about the hunt.
   passion/passionate

6. But each showed his _____ in a different way.
   passion/passionately

7. The storm winds blew the waves to a _____ height.
   terrifying/terrifyingly

8. But the men felt excitement rather than _____.
   terror/terrifying

Extension Activity

Learn More about Whales

In "The Whale Hunt," you read about whalers who traveled off the coast of Massachusetts. They hunted whales mostly for their oil.

A. Read about whales.

Whales are mammals. Like people, cats, and other mammals, whales give birth to live babies and feed their babies milk. Whales do not breathe using gills, as fish do. Whales breathe using lungs. To fill their lungs with air, whales must come to the surface of the water regularly. Sperm whales—the ones in this story—can hold their breath under water for up to 2 hours.

There are many kinds of whales. Scientists believe that the blue whale is the largest animal that ever lived. Sperm whales are not as big as blue whales, but they are the largest toothed whales.

B. Make a diagram, or labeled picture, of a whale. Follow these steps:

1. Use the Internet or library books to find out more about whales.

2. Draw a picture of the kind of whale that you like best.

3. Write the name of the whale at the top of the page.

4. Label the different parts of the whale.

Writing Practice

Write a Journal Entry

People write in **journals** to record their thoughts and feelings about things that happen to them. Each piece of writing in a journal is called an **entry.** Entries usually begin with the date.

Imagine that Ishmael kept a journal. His entry may have been something like this.

May 3, 1848

I was working with ropes as we sailed along. Suddenly I heard Tashtego yelling. He had spotted a group of whales! Quickly, we set off in small boats. We rowed toward the whales, but they disappeared under the water.

A storm was growing. We chased a whale, and Queequeg threw his harpoon. The whale came up under our boat, throwing us into the sea. We managed to save ourselves. We spent the night in the boat with water up to our knees. In the morning we swam to the Pequod.

Write a journal entry of your own. Write about what happened to you yesterday or today. Include only the most important events. Since this journal is not private, include only information you would want another person to read.

Paste

Adapted from the story by Henry James

Before You Read

About "Paste"

Characters
Charlotte, a governess; Arthur Prime, her cousin; Mrs. Guy, a friend of the family with whom Charlotte lives

Plot
When Charlotte's stepaunt dies, Charlotte receives the lady's costume jewelry as a remembrance. Among the fake jewels is a pearl necklace. When Charlotte learns that the pearls are real, she must decide what to do.

Setting
Time: around 1900
Place: the home of Arthur's father; the home where Charlotte works

Theme
Just as it is hard to tell real jewels from fake jewels, it is hard to tell real friends from false friends.

Build Background

Telling Real from False

The word *paste,* the story's title, has several meanings. It can mean the soft mixture used to glue paper or clean teeth. The paste in this story is a mixture used to make fake, or false, jewelry. This story is about telling real jewelry from false jewelry. It is also about telling real friends from false friends.

What reasons might a person have for pretending to be someone's friend?

Key Words

Read these sentences. Try to understand each word in dark type by looking at the other words in the sentence. Use a dictionary to check your ideas. Write each word and its meaning in your notebook.

1. **False** pearls can look a lot like real pearls, but they are not worth much money.

2. They held the **funeral** service a day after the woman died.

3. Charlotte was a **governess.** She cared for the children of a wealthy couple.

4. Her cousin's **greed** made him keep everything of value for himself.

5. The **pearl necklace** felt so heavy around Charlotte's neck that Charlotte thought the pearls might be real.

Reading Strategy

Identify Causes and Effects

Identifying causes and effects as you read can help you better understand a story. A short story tells about events that happen. What happens is an **effect**. Why it happens is the **cause**.

Here are examples:

Cause: Charlotte had no money of her own.

Effect: Charlotte worked as a governess for a wealthy family.

Cause: Arthur thought the pearls were not valuable.

Effect: He gave the pearls to Charlotte.

As you read, look for causes and effects. In other words, look for the important events and the reasons why they happened. This will help you understand the story better.

Paste

Adapted from the story by Henry James

I

I've found a lot more of her things," Charlotte's cousin said to her after his stepmother's funeral. "They're up in her room—but they're things I wish you'd look at."

Charlotte and her cousin, Arthur Prime, were waiting for lunch in the garden of Arthur's father, who had been a country minister. It seemed to Charlotte that Arthur's face showed the wish to express some kind of feeling. It was not surprising that Arthur should feel something. His stepmother had recently died, only three weeks after his father's death.

Charlotte had no money of her own and lived with a wealthy family as governess for their children. She had asked for leave to attend the funeral. During her stay Charlotte had noticed that her cousin seemed somehow to grieve without sorrow, to suffer without pain. It was Arthur's habit to drop a comment and leave her to pick it up without help. What "things" did he mean now? However, since she hoped for a remembrance of her stepaunt, she went to look at these "things" he had spoken of.

As she entered the darkened room, Charlotte's eyes were struck by the bright jewels that glowed on the table. Even before touching them, she guessed they were things of the theater. They were much too fine to have been things of a minister's wife. Her stepaunt had worn no jewelry to speak of, and these were crowns and necklaces, diamonds and gold. After her first shock, Charlotte picked them up. They seemed like proof of the far-off, faded story of her stepaunt's life. Her uncle, a country minister, had lost his first wife. With a small son, Arthur, and a large admiration for the theater, he had developed an even larger admiration for an unknown actress. He had offered his hand in marriage. Still more surprisingly, the actress had accepted. Charlotte had suspected for years that her stepaunt's acting could not have brought her either fame or fortune.

"You see what it is—old stuff of the time she never liked to mention."

Charlotte jumped a little. Arthur must have followed her upstairs. He was watching her slightly nervous recognition of the jewelry.

"I thought so myself," she replied. Then, to show intelligence without sounding silly, she said, "How odd they look!"

"They look awful," said Arthur Prime. "Cheap glass diamonds as big as potatoes. Actors have better taste now."

"Oh," said Charlotte, wanting to sound as knowledgeable as he, "now actresses have real diamonds."

"Some of them do."

"Oh, I mean even the bad ones—the nobodies, too."

Arthur replied coldly, "Some of the nobodies have the biggest jewels. But Mama wasn't *that* sort of actress."

"A nobody?" Charlotte asked.

"She wasn't a nobody that someone would give—well, not a nobody with diamonds. This stuff is worthless."

There was something about the old theater pieces that attracted Charlotte. She continued to turn them over in her hands.

Arthur paused, then he asked: "Do you care for them? I mean, as a remembrance?"

"Of you?" Charlotte said quickly.

"Of me? What do I have to do with it? Of your poor, dead aunt, who was so kind to you," he said virtuously.

"Well, I would rather have them than nothing."

"Then please take them." His face expressed more hope than generosity.

"Thank you." Charlotte lifted two or three pieces up and then set them down again. They were light, but so large and fake that they made an awkward gift.

"Did you know she had kept them?"

"I don't believe she knew they were there, and I'm sure my father didn't. Her connection with the theater was over. These things were just put in a corner and forgotten."

Charlotte wondered, "What corner had she found to put them in?"

"She hadn't *found* it, she'd lost it," Arthur insisted. "The whole thing had passed from her mind after she put the stuff into a box in the schoolroom cupboard. The box had been stuck there for years."

"Are you sure they're not worth anything?" Charlotte asked dreamily.

But Arthur Prime had already asked himself this question and found the answer.

"If they had been worth anything, she would have sold them long ago. Unfortunately, my father and she were never wealthy enough to keep things of value locked up."

He looked at Charlotte for agreement and added, like one who is unfamiliar with generosity, "And if they're worth anything at all— why, you're all the more welcome to them."

Charlotte picked up a small silk bag. As she opened it she answered him, "I shall like them. They're all I have."

"All you have—?"

"That belonged to her."

He looked around the poor room as if to question her greed. "Well, what else do you want?"

"Nothing. Thank you very much." As she said this she looked into the small silk bag. It held a necklace of large pearls.

"Perhaps this is worth something. Feel it." She passed him the necklace.

He weighed it in his hands without interest. "Worthless, I'm sure—it's paste."

"But is it paste?"

He spoke impatiently. "Pearls nearly as large as nuts?"

"But they're heavy," Charlotte insisted.

"No heavier than anything else," he said, as if amused at her simplicity.

Charlotte studied them a little, feeling them, turning them around.

"Couldn't they possibly be real?"

"Of that size? Put away with that stuff?"

"Well, I admit it's not likely," Charlotte said. "And pearls are so easily imitated."

"Pearls are *not* easily imitated, to anyone who knows about them. These have no shine. Anyway, how would she have got them?"

"Couldn't they have been a present?" Charlotte asked.

Arthur looked at her as if she had said something improper. "You mean because actresses are approached by men who—" He stopped suddenly. "No, they couldn't have been a present," he said sharply, and left the room.

Later, in the evening, they met to discuss Charlotte's departure the next day. At the end of the conversation, Arthur said, "I really can't let you think that my stepmother was at *any* time of her life a woman who could—"

"Accept expensive presents from admirers?" Charlotte added.

Somehow Arthur always made her speak more directly than she meant to. But he only answered, seriously, "Exactly."

"I didn't think of that, when I spoke this morning," said Charlotte apologetically, "but I see what you mean."

"I mean that her virtue was above question," said Arthur Prime.

"A hundred times yes."

"Therefore she could never have afforded such pearls on her small salary."

"Of *course* she couldn't," Charlotte answered comfortingly. "Anyway," she continued, "I noticed that the clasp that holds the pearls together isn't even gold. I suppose it wouldn't be, with false pearls."

"The whole thing is cheap paste," Arthur announced, as if to end their discussion. "If the pearls were *real,* and she had hidden them all these years—"

"Yes?" asked Charlotte curiously.

"Well, I wouldn't know *what* to think!"

"Oh, I see," said Charlotte, and their conversation ended.

II

When she was back at work again, the false jewels seemed silly to Charlotte. She wasn't sure why she had taken them. She put them away under a pile of clothing, and there they might have stayed, except for the arrival of Mrs. Guy.

Mrs. Guy was a strange little woman with red hair and black dresses. She had the face of a baby, but took command like a general. She was a friend of the family Charlotte worked for. She had come to organize a week of parties to celebrate the twenty-first birthday of the family's oldest son. She happily accepted Charlotte's help with the entertainments.

"Tomorrow and Thursday are all right, but we need to plan something for Friday evening," she announced to Charlotte.

"What would you like to do?"

"Well, plays are my strong point, you know," said Mrs. Guy.

They discussed plays and looked at the hats and dresses they might wear.

"But we need something to brighten these up," Mrs. Guy decided. "These things are too dull. Haven't you got anything else?"

"Well, I do have a few things . . ." Charlotte admitted slowly. She went to find the jewels for Mrs. Guy. "Perhaps they're too bright, they're just glass and paste."

"Larger than life!" Mrs. Guy was excited. "They are just what we need. They'll give me great ideas!"

The next morning she came to find Charlotte in the schoolroom.

"I don't understand where you got these pieces," she said to Charlotte.

"They belonged to my aunt, who died a few months ago. She was an actress for several years. They were part of her theatrical equipment."

"She left them to you?"

"No; my cousin, her stepson, who naturally has no use for them, gave them to me as a remembrance of her. She was a dear, kind person, always so nice to me, and I was very fond of her."

Mrs. Guy listened with interest. "But it must be your *cousin* who is a 'dear, kind person.' Is *he* also 'always so nice' to you?"

"What do you mean?" asked Charlotte.

"Can't you guess?"

A strange feeling came over Charlotte. "The pearls—" she started to say.

"Doesn't your cousin know either?"

Charlotte felt herself turning pink. "They're *not* paste?"

"Haven't you looked at them?" Mrs. Guy continued.

Charlotte felt ashamed. Not to have known that the pearls were real!

"Come to my room when you finish teaching," Mrs. Guy ordered, "You'll see!"

Later, in Mrs. Guy's room, Charlotte stared at the pearls around Mrs. Guy's neck. Surely they were the only mysterious thing her stepaunt had owned.

"What in the world have you done to them?"

"I only handled them, understood them, admired them and put them on," Mrs. Guy answered proudly. "That's what pearls need. They need to be worn—it wakes them up. They're alive, you see. How have these been treated? They must have been buried, ignored. They were half dead. Don't you know about pearls?"

"How could I have known?" said penniless Charlotte. "Do you?"

"I know everything about pearls. These were simply asleep. From the moment I touched them you could see they were real."

"I couldn't see," admitted Charlotte, "although I did wonder about them. Then their value—"

"Oh, their value is excellent!"

Charlotte felt dizzy. "But my cousin didn't know. He thinks they're worthless."

"Because the rest of the jewels are fake? Then your cousin is a fool. But, anyway, he gave them to you."

"But if he gave them to me because he thought they were worthless—"

"You think you must give them back? I don't agree. If he was such a fool that he didn't recognize their value, it's his fault."

Charlotte looked at the pearls. They *were* beautiful. At the moment, however, they seemed to belong more to Mrs. Guy than to Charlotte or her cousin. She said finally: "Yes, he insisted that the pearls were paste, even after I clearly said they looked different from the other things."

"Well, then, you see!" said Mrs. Guy. Her voice expressed more than victory over Arthur Prime—she sounded relieved.

But Charlotte was still not sure. "You see, he thought they couldn't be different because they shouldn't be."

"Shouldn't be? I don't understand."

"Well, how would she have got them?" Charlotte asked directly.

"Do you mean she might have stolen them?"

"No, but she had been an actress."

"Well, then!" cried Mrs. Guy. "That's exactly how she got them."

"Yes, but she wasn't famous or rich."

"Was she ugly?" Mrs. Guy inquired.

"No. She must have looked rather nice when she was young."

"Well, then!" cried Mrs. Guy again, as if she had proved her point.

"You mean the pearls were a present? That's just the idea my cousin dislikes—that she had such a generous admirer."

"And that she wouldn't have taken the pearls for nothing? I should think not! Let's hope she gave him something in return. Let's hope she was kind to him."

"Well," Charlotte continued, "I suppose she must have been 'kind' as you call it. That's why none of us knew she had something so valuable. That's why she had to hide them."

"You're suggesting that she was ashamed of them?"

"Well, she had married a minister."

"But he married *her*. What did he think of her past life?"

"Well, that she was not the sort of woman who encouraged such gifts."

"Ah! my dear! What woman is *not!*" said Mrs. Guy with a smile.

"And I don't want to give away her secret," continued Charlotte. "I liked her very much."

"Then don't!" decided Mrs. Guy. "Keep them."

"It's so difficult!" sighed Charlotte. "I must think. I'll tell you tonight, after I decide what to do."

"But may I wear them—this evening at dinner?" Mrs. Guy's hands held the pearls lovingly.

It was probably Mrs. Guy's possessiveness that decided Charlotte; but for the moment she only said, "As you like," before she left the room.

It was almost eleven o'clock before Charlotte had a chance to meet with Mrs. Guy again that evening. Mrs. Guy had worn the pearls to dinner, and announced that they had been "A great success, my dear, a sensation!"

"They are beautiful," Charlotte agreed, "but I can't be silent."

"Then you plan to return them?"

"If I don't, I'll be a thief."

"If you do, you're a fool!" said Mrs. Guy angrily.

"Well, of the two . . ." Charlotte answered faintly.

Mrs. Guy interrupted her. "You won't tell him I told you that they're real, will you?"

"No, certainly not."

"Then, perhaps he won't believe you, and he will give them back to us!" And feeling much better, Mrs. Guy went to bed.

But Charlotte didn't like to return the pearls to Arthur Prime by mail, and was too busy to go to town herself. On the last day of Mrs. Guy's visit, she came to Charlotte.

"Come now, how much will you sell them for?"

"The pearls? Oh, you'll have to bargain with my cousin."

"Where does he live?"

Charlotte gave her the address.

"But how can I talk with him if you don't do anything about returning them?" Mrs. Guy complained.

"Oh, I *will*. I'm only waiting until the family goes to town. Do you want the pearls so much?"

"I'm dying for them. There's a special mystery about them. They have a white glow." Mrs. Guy paused. "My dear," she whispered, "they're things of love!"

"Oh, dear!" cried Charlotte.

"They're things of passion!"

"Oh, heavens!"

III

Mrs. Guy left, but Charlotte couldn't forget her words. She felt she had a new view of her dear, dead aunt. Had her stepaunt suffered over the pearls, hidden away with the false jewels? Charlotte began wearing the pearls in private; she came to feel a strange attachment to them. But still she was poor, and she dreamed that Arthur Prime might show an uncharacteristic generosity and say to her: "Oh, keep the pearls! Of course, I couldn't afford to give them to you if I had known their value. But since you *have* got them, and found out the truth yourself, I really can't take them away from you."

In fact, his reaction was quite different when she finally went to town to tell him her story.

"I don't believe in them," he said. He was angry and pale.

"That's exactly what I wanted to hear," Charlotte replied.

"It's a most unpleasant, improper suggestion," he added. "To think that she . . ."

"If you're afraid to believe they're real, it's not my fault."

Arthur said nothing for a while. Then he picked them up. "They're what I said originally. They're only paste."

"Then may I keep them?"

"No. I want a better opinion."

"Better than your opinion."

"No. Better than *yours*." Arthur took the pearls and locked them in a drawer.

"You say I'm afraid," he added. "But I won't be afraid to take them to a jeweler to ask for an opinion."

"And if he says they're real?"

"He won't say so. He couldn't," Arthur insisted.

Two weeks later Charlotte received a letter about the pearls from Arthur. Still later Mrs. Guy was invited to dinner by Charlotte's employer. She was wearing a beautiful string of pearls.

"Do you see?" She came over to greet Charlotte, pointing at her necklace.

Charlotte wore a sickly smile. "They're almost as nice as Arthur's," she said.

"Almost? Where are your eyes, my dear? They *are* Arthur's. I tracked them to the jeweler's window where he sold them."

"*Sold* them?" Charlotte was horrified. "He wrote me that I had insulted his stepmother and that the jeweler had shown him that he was right—he said the pearls were only paste!"

Mrs. Guy stared at her. "Ah, I told you he wouldn't believe you."

"He wrote me," Charlotte continued, full of her private wrong, "that he had smashed them."

"He is really very disturbed." Mrs. Guy's voice expressed pity and wonder.

But it was not quite clear whom she pitied, Arthur or Charlotte. And Charlotte felt disturbed, too, when she thought about it later. Had Mrs. Guy really tracked the pearls to a jeweler's window? Or had she dealt with Arthur directly? Charlotte remembered clearly that she had given Mrs. Guy his address. ⌒

After You Read

Understand the Story

Answer these questions in your notebook. Write complete sentences.

1. What did Arthur ask Charlotte to do after his stepmother's funeral?

2. What were the "things" that Charlotte found in her stepaunt's room? Describe them.

3. What did Charlotte find in the small silk bag?

4. Why did Charlotte let Mrs. Guy wear the pearls to dinner?

5. Why did Charlotte start wearing the pearls in private?

6. In the end, where did Mrs. Guy say she got the pearls? Where else may she have gotten them?

Elements of Literature

Foreshadowing

Foreshadowing is giving the reader clues about what will happen. Authors use foreshadowing to invite the reader to predict how the story will end. This makes the reader keep reading, curious to see whether his or her prediction is correct. Read this passage from the story. Then answer the questions.

> Charlotte looked at the pearls. They *were* beautiful. At the moment, however, they seemed to belong more to Mrs. Guy than to Charlotte or her cousin. She said finally: "Yes, he insisted that the pearls were paste, even after I clearly said they looked different from the other things."

How does the author use foreshadowing in the passage above? How do the author's clues make the reader want to keep reading?

Discussion

Answer the questions in pairs or small groups.

1. Charlotte finally takes the pearls back to Arthur. She hopes he will let her keep them. Instead, he locks them in a drawer. He says he will take them to a jeweler. But he also says he is sure the jeweler will say they are paste. Why, then, does Arthur keep them? Why doesn't he let Charlotte keep the pearls, if he's so sure they are not real?

2. When Mrs. Guy learns from Charlotte about Arthur's letter, she expresses "pity and wonder." But we are told that "it was not quite clear whom she pitied, Arthur or Charlotte." What reasons might Mrs. Guy have for pitying Arthur? What reasons might she have for pitying Charlotte?

Vocabulary

Choose the correct word. Write the completed sentences in your notebook.

1. Charlotte looked into the small silk bag. Inside was a _____.
   a. funeral   **b.** governess   **c.** pearl necklace

2. The pearls were heavy. They did not seem _____.
   a. real   **b.** false   **c.** greed

3. Arthur gave Charlotte the jewels after his stepmother's _____.
   a. funeral   **b.** greed   **c.** wedding

4. Charlotte worked as _____ for the children of a wealthy couple.
   a. stepaunt   **b.** actress   **c.** governess

5. Arthur's _____ caused him to give Charlotte jewels he thought were worthless.
   a. greed   **b.** funeral   **c.** governess

Word Study

Write the sentences below in your notebook. Complete each sentence with the correct form of the word. Use the chart to help you. The first item has been done for you.

Adjective	Adverb
angry	angrily
surprising	surprisingly
disturbing	disturbingly
generous	generously
loving	lovingly
proud	proudly

1. "If you return the pearls, you're a fool!" said Mrs. Guy
   _____angrily_____.
   angry/angrily

2. It was not _____ that Arthur should feel
   surprising/surprisingly
   something. His stepmother had recently died.

3. The fact that Arthur had lied was _____ to
   disturbing/disturbingly
   Charlotte, but not to Mrs. Guy.

4. Arthur was not a _____ man.
   generous/generously

5. Mrs. Guy's hands held the pearls _____.
   loving/lovingly

6. "These pearls look beautiful on me," Mrs. Guy said
   _____ as she looked at herself in the mirror.
   proud/proudly

Extension Activity

Learn More about Pearls

In "Paste," the necklace was made of real pearls. Pearls, like other jewels, are valuable because they are not easy to find or get.

A. Read about pearls and oysters.

Pearls are found inside oysters. When a grain of sand gets inside an oyster, it irritates the oyster. The oyster produces a chemical that covers the grain of sand. The chemical is called *nacre*. Nacre builds up and turns the grain of sand into a pearl.

Throughout history, pearls have been thought of as valuable jewelry. Today, many pearls are cultured. A person purposely opens the shell of an oyster and places something irritating inside. The pearl that is formed is called a cultured pearl. Cultured pearls are not as valuable as pearls that form naturally.

B. Make a poster about a material used to make jewelry. You may choose materials such as diamonds or gold. Follow these steps:

1. Choose a jewel or precious metal that interests you.

2. Use library books, an encyclopedia, or the Internet to find information about the material.

3. Take notes as you read.

4. On poster board, draw a picture of jewelry made with the material. Write facts about the material around your picture.

5. Share your poster with your classmates.

Before You Read

About "The Lost Phoebe"

Characters
Henry Reifsneider; Phoebe, Henry's wife

Plot
Henry and his wife Phoebe had been married for forty-eight years. They lived a simple, predictable life. After Phoebe's death, Henry is alone. Henry learns how to live on his own in a most unusual way.

Setting
Time: early 1900s
Place: the Reifsneider home in Watersville, a farming community

Theme
The human mind can create its own reality when reality is too painful.

Build Background

Country Ways
The story you will read is about a couple who lived in a country community a century ago. Most people in such communities kept small farms. Their lives revolved around their farm work. They followed certain patterns of daily life that did not change much from year to year. There was little free time, not much money, and few choices. Neighbors in these communities tried to help one another in times of need.

Would you like to live in a farming community? Why or why not?

Key Words

Read these sentences. Try to understand each word in dark type by looking at the other words in the sentence. Use a dictionary to check your ideas. Write each word and its meaning in your notebook.

<table>
<tr><td></td><td>astonished</td></tr>
<tr><td></td><td>fond</td></tr>
<tr><td></td><td>hallucination</td></tr>
<tr><td></td><td>old fashioned</td></tr>
<tr><td></td><td>sympathetic</td></tr>
</table>

1. Henry was greatly surprised, really **astonished,** when he thought he saw a ghost.

2. Henry's neighbors were quite **fond** of him. They knew him well and liked him.

3. Henry had a **hallucination**, seeing something that was not really there.

4. The furniture in Henry's house was **old fashioned,** made a long time ago.

5. Henry's neighbors were **sympathetic.** They were kind and very understanding of Henry's behavior.

Reading Strategy

Monitor Comprehension

Monitor, or check, your **comprehension** as you read. For example, ask yourself, "Did I understand that paragraph? What didn't I understand?" If you find a part of a story that you don't understand, follow these steps:

- Reread that part of the story.

- Try to retell that part of the story in your own words.

- Write questions about things that you don't understand.

- Look back through the story for answers to your questions or ask your teacher.

The Lost Phoebe

Adapted from the story by Theodore Dreiser

I

Old Henry Reifsneider and his wife Phoebe had lived together for forty-eight years. They had lived three miles from a small town whose population was steadily falling. This part of the country was not as wealthy as it used to be. It wasn't thickly settled, either. Perhaps there was a house every mile or so, with fields in between. Their own house had been built by Henry's grandfather many years ago. A new part had been added to the original log cabin when Henry married Phoebe. The new part was now weather-beaten. Wind whistled through cracks in the boards. Large, lovely trees surrounded the house. But they made it seem a little damp inside.

The furniture, like the house, was old. There was a tall cupboard of cherry wood and a large, old-fashioned bed. The chest of drawers was also high and wide and solidly built. But it had faded, and smelled damp. The carpet that lay under the strong, lasting furniture had been made by Phoebe herself, fifteen years before she died. Now it was worn and faded to a dull gray and pink. The frame that she had made the carpet on was still there. It stood like a dusty, bony skeleton in the east room. All sorts of broken-down furniture lay around the place. There was a doorless clothes cupboard. A broken mirror hung in an old cherry wood frame. It had fallen from a nail and cracked three days before their youngest son, Jerry, died. There was a hat stand whose china knobs had broken off. And an old-fashioned sewing machine.

The orchard to the east of the house was full of rotting apple trees. Their twisted branches were covered with greenish-white moss which looked sad and ghostly in the moonlight. Besides the orchard, several low buildings surrounded the house. They had once housed chickens, a horse or two, a cow, and several pigs. The same gray-green moss covered their roofs. They had not been painted for so long that they had turned a grayish-black. In fact, everything on the farm had aged and faded along with Old Henry and his wife Phoebe.

They had lived here, these two, since their marriage forty-eight years before. And Henry had lived here as a child. His father and mother had been old when Henry married. They had invited him to bring his wife to the farm. They had all lived together for ten years before his mother and father died. After that Henry and Phoebe were left alone with their four children. But all sorts of things had happened since then. They had had seven children, but three had died. One girl had gone to Kansas. One boy had gone to Sioux Falls and was never even heard from again. Another boy had gone to Washington. The last girl lived five counties away in the same state. She had so many problems of her own, however, that she rarely gave her parents a thought. Their very ordinary home life had never been attractive to the children. So time had drawn them away. Wherever they were, they gave little thought to their father and mother.

Old Henry Reifsneider and his wife Phoebe were a loving couple. You perhaps know how it is with such simple people. They fasten themselves like moss on stones, until they and their circumstances are worn away. The larger world has no call to them; or if it does, they don't hear it. The orchard, the fields, the pigpen, and the chicken house measure the range of their human activities. When the wheat is ripe, it is harvested. When the corn is full, it is cut. After that comes winter. The grain is taken to market, the wood is cut for the fires. The work is simple: fire-building, meal-getting, occasional repairing, visiting. There are also changes in the weather—the snow, the rains, and the fair days. Beyond these things, nothing else means very much. All the rest of life is a far-off dream. It shines, far away, like starlight. It sounds as faint as cowbells in the distance.

Old Henry and his wife Phoebe were as fond of each other as is possible for two old people who have nothing else in this life to be fond of. He was a thin old man, seventy when she died. He was a

strange, moody person with thick, uncombed gray-black hair and beard. He looked at you out of dull, fish-like watery eyes. His clothes, like the clothes of many farmers, were old and ill-fitting. They were too large at the neck. The knees and elbows were stretched and worn. Phoebe was thin and shapeless. Dressed in black, she looked like an umbrella. As time had passed they had only themselves to look after. Their activities had become fewer and fewer. The herd of pigs was reduced to one. The sleepy horse Henry still kept was neither very clean nor well-fed. Almost all the chickens had disappeared. They had been killed by animals or disease. The once-healthy vegetable garden was now only a memory of itself. The flower beds were overgrown. A will had been made which divided the small property equally among the remaining four children. It was so small that it was really of no interest to any of them. Yet

Henry and Phoebe lived together in peace and sympathy. Once in a while Old Henry would become moody and annoyed. He would complain that something unimportant had been lost.

"Phoebe, where's my corn knife? You never leave my things alone."

"Now you be quiet, Henry," his wife would answer in her old cracked voice. "If you don't, I'll leave you. I'll get up and walk out of here one day. Then where would you be? You don't have anybody but me to look after you, so just behave yourself. Your corn knife is in the cupboard where it's always been, unless you put it somewhere else."

Old Henry knew his wife would never leave him. But sometimes he wondered what he would do if she died. That was the one leaving he was afraid of. Every night he wound the old clock and went to lock the doors, and it comforted him to know Phoebe was in bed. If he moved in his sleep she would be there to ask him what he wanted.

"Now, Henry, do lie still! You're as restless as a chicken."

"Well, I can't sleep, Phoebe."

"Well, you don't have to roll over so much. You can let me sleep." This would usually put him to sleep.

If she wanted a pail of water, he complained, but it gave him pleasure to bring it. If she rose first to build the fire, he made sure the wood was cut and placed within easy reach. So they divided this simple world nicely between them.

II

In the spring of her sixty-fourth year, Phoebe became sick. Old Henry drove to town and brought back the doctor. But because of her age, her sickness was not curable, and one cold night she died. Henry could have gone to live with his youngest daughter. But it was really too much trouble. He was too weary and used to his home. He wanted to remain near where they had put his Phoebe.

His neighbors invited him to stay with them. But he didn't want to. So his friends left him with advice and offers of help. They sent supplies of coffee and bacon and bread. He tried to interest himself in farming to keep himself busy. But it was sad to come into the house in the evening. He could find no shadow of Phoebe, although everything in the house suggested her. At night he read the newspapers that friends had left for him. Or he read his Bible, which he had forgotten about for years. But he could get little comfort from these things. Mostly he sat and wondered where Phoebe had gone, and how soon he would die.

He made coffee every morning and fried himself some bacon at night. But he wasn't hungry. His house was empty; its shadows saddened him. So he lived quite unhappily for five long months. And then a change began.

It was a moonlight night. The moss-covered orchard shone ghostly silver. As usual, Henry was thinking of Phoebe and the years when they had been young together. And he thought about the children who had gone. The condition of the house was becoming worse. The sheets were not clean, because he made a poor job of the laundry. The roof leaked, and things inside got damp. But he didn't do anything about it. He preferred to walk slowly back and forth, or sit and think.

By 12:00 midnight of this particular night, however, he was asleep. He woke up at 2:00. The moon shone in through the living room windows. His coat lying on the back of the chair made a shadow near the table. It looked like Phoebe as she used to sit there. Could it be she—or her ghost? He never used to believe in spirits, and yet . . . He stared at it in the pale light. His old hair seemed to rise up from his head. He sat up, but the figure did not move. He put his thin legs out of the bed. He wondered if this could really be Phoebe. They had often talked about ghosts and spirits. But they had never agreed that such things could be. His wife had never believed that her spirit could return to walk the earth. She had believed in a heaven where good folk would want to stay and not come back. Yet here she was now, bending over the table. She was wearing her black dress. Her face shone pale in the moonlight.

"Phoebe," he called, excited from head to toe. "Have you come back?"

The figure did not move. He got up and walked uncertainly toward the door, watching it carefully. As he came near, however, the ghost became once more his coat upon the chair.

"Well," he said to himself, his mouth open in wonder, "I surely thought I saw her." He ran his hands through his hair while his excitement relaxed. Although it had disappeared, he had the idea that she might return.

Another night he looked out of the window toward the chicken house and pigpen. Mist was rising from the damp ground, and he thought he saw Phoebe. She always used to cross from the kitchen door to the pigpen to feed the pigs. And here she was again. He sat up and watched her. He was doubtful because of the first experience. But his body shook with excitement. Perhaps there really were spirits. Phoebe must be worried about his loneliness. She must be thinking about him. He watched her until a breath of wind blew the mist away.

A third night, as he was dreaming, she came to his bed.

"Poor Henry," she said. "It's too bad." He woke up and thought he saw her move from the bedroom into the living room. He got up, greatly astonished. He was sure that Phoebe was coming back to him. If he thought about her enough, if he showed her how much he needed her, she would come back. She would tell him what to do. Perhaps she would stay with him most of the time. At least, during the night. That would make him less lonely.

For the old or weak, imagination may easily develop into actual hallucination. Eventually this change happened for Henry. Night after night he waited, expecting her return. Once in a strange mood he thought he saw a pale light moving about the room. Another time he saw her walking in the orchard after dark. Then one morning he felt he could not bear his loneliness any longer. He woke up with the knowledge that she was not dead. It is hard to say how he felt so certain. His mind was gone. In its place was the hallucination that he and Phoebe had had a senseless quarrel. He had complained that she had moved his pipe. In the past she had jokingly threatened to leave him if he did not behave himself.

"I guess I could find you again," he had always said. But her joking threat had always been the same:

"You won't find me if I ever leave you. I guess I can get to some place where you can't find me."

When he got up that morning he didn't build the fire or cut the bread as usual. He began to think where he should look for her. He put on his soft hat and took his walking stick from behind the door. He started out energetically to look for her among his neighbors. His old shoes scratched loudly in the dust. His gray hair, now grown rather long, hung down below his hat. His hands and face were pale.

"Why, hello, Henry! Where are you going this morning?" inquired Farmer Dodge.

"You haven't seen Phoebe, have you?"

"Phoebe who?" asked Farmer Dodge. He didn't connect the name with Henry's dead wife.

"Why, my wife, Phoebe, of course. Who do you suppose I mean?"

"Oh, come on, Henry! You aren't joking, are you? It can't be your wife you're talking about. She's dead."

"Dead? Not Phoebe! She left me early this morning while I was sleeping. We had a little quarrel last night, and I guess that's the reason. But I guess I can find her. She's gone over to Matilda Race's, that's where she's gone."

He started quickly up the road. The astonished Dodge stared after him. "Well!" he said to himself. "He's gone crazy. That poor old man has lived down there alone until he's gone completely out of his mind. I'll have to inform the police."

"Why, Mr. Reifsneider," cried old Matilda Race as Henry knocked on her door. "What brings you here this morning?"

"Is Phoebe here?" he demanded eagerly.

"Phoebe who? What Phoebe?" replied Mrs. Race, curious.

"Why, my Phoebe, of course, my wife Phoebe. Who do you suppose? Isn't she here now?"

"Why, you poor man!" cried Mrs. Race. "You've lost your mind. You come right in and sit down. I'll get you a cup of coffee. Of course your wife isn't here. But you come in and sit down. I'll find her for you after a while. I know where she is."

The old farmer's eyes softened at her sympathy.

"We had a quarrel last night and she left me," Henry offered.

"Oh, my!" Mrs. Race sighed to herself. There was no one there to share her astonishment. "The poor man! Now somebody's just got to look after him. He can't be allowed to run around the country this way looking for his dead wife. It's terrible."

She boiled him a pot of coffee and brought in some new-baked bread and fresh butter. She put on a couple of eggs to boil, lying as she spoke: "Now, you stay right there, Henry, until Jake comes in. I'll send him to look for Phoebe. I think she must be over at Sumnerton with some of her friends. Anyhow, we'll find out. Now you just drink this coffee and eat this bread. You must be tired. You've had a long walk this morning." Her idea was to wait for her husband, Jake, and perhaps have him call the police.

Henry ate, but his mind was on his wife. Since she was not here, perhaps she was visiting the Murrays—miles away in another direction. He decided that he would not wait for Jake Race. He would search for his wife himself.

"Well, I'll be going," he said, getting up and looking strangely about him. "I guess she didn't come here after all. She went over to the Murrays', I guess." And he marched out, ignoring Matilda Race's cries of worry.

Two hours later his dusty, eager figure appeared in the Murrays' doorway. He had walked five miles and it was noon. The Murrays, a husband and wife of sixty, listened to him with astonishment. They also realized that he was mad. They invited him to stay to dinner. They intended to call the police later, to see what could be done. But Henry did not stay long. His need for Phoebe pulled him off to another distant farmhouse. So it went for that day and the next and the next. And the circle of his questioning grew wider and wider.

And although Henry came to many doors, and the police were informed, it was decided not to send him to the county hospital. The condition of mad patients in this hospital was horrifying. It was found that Henry returned peaceably to his lonely home at night to see if his wife had returned. Who would lock up a thin, eager, old man with gray hair and a kindly, innocent, inquiring manner? His neighbors had known him as a kindly, dependable man. He could do no harm. Many people gave him food and old clothes—at least at first. His figure became a common sight, and the answer, "Why no, Henry, I haven't seen her," or, "No, Henry, she hasn't been here today," became more customary.

III

For several years afterward he was an odd figure in the sun and rain, on dusty roads and muddy ones. The longer he walked in this manner, the deeper his strange hallucination became. He found it harder and harder to return from his more and more distant searches. Finally he began to take a few eating utensils with him so he would not have to return home at night. In an old coffeepot he put a small tin cup. He took a knife, fork, and spoon, and salt and pepper. He tied a tin plate to the pot. It was no trouble for him to get the little food he needed. And with a strange, almost religious manner, he didn't hesitate to ask for that much. Slowly his hair became longer and longer. His black hat became an earthen brown, and his clothes worn and dusty.

For three years he walked with only his clothes, his stick, and his utensils. No one knew how far he went, or how he lived through the storms and cold. They did not see him find shelter in piles of grass or by the sides of cattle. The warm bodies of the cows protected him

from cold, and their dull minds did not oppose his presence. Overhanging rocks and trees kept him from the rain.

The progress of such hallucinations is strange. He had asked for Phoebe at people's doors and got no answer. Finally he decided that she was not in any of the houses. But she might be within reach of his voice. So he began to call sad, occasional cries. "O-o-o Phoebe! O-o-o Phoebe!" waked the quiet countryside and echoed through the hills. It had a sad, mad ring. Many farmers recognized it from far away and said, "There goes old Reifsneider."

Sometimes when he reached a crossroad, he couldn't decide which way to go. He developed another hallucination to help him. He believed Phoebe's spirit or some power of the air or wind or nature would tell him where to go. He would stand at the crossroad and close his eyes. He would turn around three times and call "O-o-o Phoebe" twice. Then he would throw his walking stick straight before him. This would surely tell him which way to go. Phoebe or some magic power would direct the stick. He would then follow the direction the stick pointed, even when it led him back the way he had come. And the hallucination that he would surely find her remained. There were hours when his feet were sore and his legs tired. There were times when he would stop in the heat to wipe his forehead, or in the cold to beat his arms. Sometimes, after throwing his stick and finding it pointing to where he had just come from, he would shake his head wearily and philosophically. He would consider for a moment the confusion and disappointment of life, and his own strange fate. Then he would start off energetically again. His strange figure finally became known in the farthest corners of three or four counties. Old Reifsneider was a sad character. His fame was wide.

About four miles from the little town called Watersville there was a place called Red Cliff. This cliff was a steep wall of red sandstone, perhaps a hundred feet high. It rose above the fruitful corn fields and orchards that lay beneath. Trees grew thickly along the top of the cliff. In fair weather it was old Reifsneider's habit to spend the night here. He would fry his bacon or boil his eggs at the foot of some tree. Then he would lie down.

He almost always woke at 2:00 in the morning. Occasionally he would walk at night. More often he would sit up and watch the darkness or the stars, wondering. Sometimes in the strangeness of his mind he imagined he saw his lost wife moving among the trees. Then he would get up to follow. He would take his utensils on a string, and his stick. When she tried to escape him he would run after her, begging. When she disappeared he would feel disappointed. He was saddened at the almost impossible difficulties of his search.

One night in the seventh year of his search he came to the top of Red Cliff. It was spring, like the spring when Phoebe had died. He had walked many many miles with his utensils, following his walking stick. It was after 10:00 at night. He was very tired. Long walking and little eating had left him only a shadow of his former self. He had little strength. Only his hallucination kept him going. He had eaten hardly anything that day. Now, exhausted, he lay down in the dark to rest and possibly sleep.

He felt the presence of his wife strongly. It would not be long now until he should see her, talk to her, he told himself. He fell asleep, after a time, his head on his knees. At midnight the moon began to rise. At 2:00 in the morning, his wakeful hour, it was a large silver ball. He opened his eyes. The moonlight made silvery patterns at his feet. The forest was full of strange light and silvery, shadowy forms. What was it that moved among the trees—a pale, shining, ghostly figure? Moonlight and shadow gave it a strange form and a stranger reality. Was it truly his lost Phoebe? It came near him. He imagined he could see her eyes. Not as she was when he last saw her in the black dress and shawl. Now she was a strangely younger Phoebe. She was the one whom he had known years before as a girl. Old Reifsneider got up. He had been expecting and dreaming of this hour all these years. Now he saw the pale light dancing before him. He looked at it questioningly, one hand on his gray hair.

For the first time in many years he suddenly remembered the full beauty of the girlish form. He saw her pleasing, sympathetic smile, her brown hair. He remembered the blue ribbon she had once worn about her waist. He saw her light and happy movements. He forgot his pots and pans and followed her. She moved before him and it seemed that she waved to him with a young and playful hand.

"Oh, Phoebe! Phoebe!" he called. "Have you really come? Have you really answered me?" On and on he hurried until he was almost running. He brushed his arms against the trees. He struck his hands and face against small branches. His hat was gone, his breath was gone, his mind quite gone when he came to the edge of the cliff. Down below he saw her among the silver apple trees now blooming in the spring.

"Oh, Phoebe!" he called. "Oh, Phoebe! Oh no, don't leave me!" He felt the pull of the world where love was young and Phoebe waited. "Oh, wait, Phoebe!" he cried, and jumped.

Some farm boys found his utensils under the tree where he had left them. Later, at the foot of the cliff, they found his body. He was pale and broken, but full of happiness. A smile of peace curved his lips. His old hat was discovered under a tree. No one of all the simple population knew how eagerly and happily he had finally found his lost Phoebe. ◠

After You Read

Understand the Story

Answer these questions in your notebook. Write complete sentences.

1. How long had Henry and Phoebe been married?

2. Had their marriage been a happy or an unhappy one? Explain.

3. How old was Henry when Phoebe died?

4. After Phoebe died, what did Henry imagine he saw?

5. Why did Henry leave home?

6. What happened to Henry on the top of Red Cliff?

Elements of Literature

Mood

Mood is the feeling the reader gets from the setting and character description. Read this passage from the story. Then answer the question that follows.

> The orchard to the east of the house was full of rotting apple trees. Their twisted branches were covered with greenish-white moss which looked sad and ghostly in the moonlight. Besides the orchard, several low buildings surrounded the house. They had once housed chickens, a horse or two, a cow, and several pigs. The same gray-green moss covered their roofs. They had not been painted for so long that they had turned a grayish-black. In fact, everything on the farm had aged and faded along with Old Henry and his wife Phoebe.

The setting and the character description in this passage create a "sad and ghostly" feeling. How does this feeling help the reader understand and appreciate the story?

Discussion

Answer the questions in pairs or small groups.

1. Despite the story's sad events, parts of it are funny. Why do you think the author included funny scenes in such a serious story?

2. What good qualities did Henry show? Are these qualities worth less in Henry than they would be in a person who was not mad? Are they worth more?

Vocabulary

Choose the correct word. Write the completed sentences in your notebook.

1. The furniture was old. There was a tall cupboard and a large, _____ bed.
   a. fond   **b.** sympathetic   **c.** old-fashioned

2. Old Henry and his wife Phoebe were _____ of each other.
   a. fond   **b.** poor   **c.** astonished

3. For the old or weak, imagination may easily develop into actual _____.
   a. moonlight   **b.** hallucination   **c.** sympathetic

4. Farmer Dodge was _____ to find Henry searching for his dead wife.
   a. astonished   **b.** hallucination   **c.** old fashioned

5. Henry saw Phoebe's pleasing, _____ smile.
   a. poor   **b.** astonished   **c.** sympathetic

Word Study

Write the sentences below in your notebook. Complete each sentence with the correct form of the word. Use the chart to help you. The first item has been done for you.

Noun	Adjective
quarrel	quarrelsome
hallucination	hallucinatory
dampness	damp
sadness	sad
astonishment	astonishing
sympathy	sympathetic

1. Henry's mind was gone. In its place was the thought that he and Phoebe had only had a senseless _____quarrel_____.
   quarrel/quarrelsome

2. Believing that Phoebe was still alive was Henry's

   _____.
   hallucination/hallucinatory

3. The roof leaked, and things inside got _____.
   dampness/damp

4. Mrs. Race was _____ about Henry's condition.
   sadness/sad

5. The Murrays listened to Henry's story with _____.
   astonishment/astonishing

6. Henry looked like a madman. But his neighbors were

   _____.
   sympathy/sympathetic

Extension Activity

About Dreams

In "The Lost Phoebe," Henry dreams about his wife. Some things can happen in dreams that couldn't possibly happen in real life.

A. Read about dreams.

Your brain is active even while you sleep. Dreams are what you imagine seeing and hearing while asleep. Everyone has dreams. But not every dream is remembered. Dreams often include people or ideas from real life. Sometimes the person who is dreaming just watches what is happening. Sometimes the dreamer is a part of the action. Some people have the same dreams again and again. These are called recurring dreams.

B. Work with a partner. Tell each other about a dream. Try to recall as much of the dream as you can. Tell which parts of the dream are from real life and which parts are not.

If you cannot remember a dream, make a list of things you would like to dream about to show your partner.

Writing Practice

Write a Descriptive Paragraph

In descriptive writing, a writer uses words to help the reader picture what a person, place, or thing looks like. When writing a story, a writer may include a description of a place to help the reader picture the story's setting.

A good descriptive paragraph about a place includes the following characteristics:

- An interesting opening to get the reader's attention
- Words that help the reader picture or imagine the place
- Details or examples

Read this description from "The Lost Phoebe":

> . . . Their own house had been built by Henry's grandfather many years ago. A new part had been added to the original log cabin when Henry married Phoebe. The new part was now weather-beaten. Wind whistled through cracks in the boards. Large, lovely trees surrounded the house. . . .

Imagine that you are going to write a short story. Choose the place where your story will begin. Write a good descriptive paragraph to describe that place.

Glossary

adjective: word that describes someone or something: *These cherries are* *sweet. Yoshi is a great cook.*

adverb: word that tells you how, when, or where something is done: *The turtle walked slowly.*

author: person who writes a story; writer

author's purpose: author's reason for writing something, such as to entertain the reader or to inform the reader

cause and effect: A cause is why something happens. An effect is what happens. A cause makes an effect happen.

characterization: how an author uses details to create a character

characters: people or animals in a story. *See* main character(s).

conflict: problem or struggle of a character in a story

description: words that describe someone or something, or tell what someone or something is like

dialogue: conversation between characters in a story

foreshadowing: an author's hints or clues about what will happen in a story

irony: when what happens is the opposite of what you expect

journal entry: piece of writing in which you tell your thoughts and feelings about events in your life

main character(s): the most important character or characters in a story. Main characters often change or learn something by the end of a story.

monitor comprehension: check to see how well you understand the story as you read

mood: feeling that a piece of writing gives you. The mood can be sad, exciting, ghostly, etc.

noun: word that names something or someone. *The bicycle is broken. My sister is a doctor.*

novel: long work of fiction that has characters, plot, setting, and sometimes a theme

opinion: a person's thoughts and feelings about a subject

personification: giving human qualities to animals or objects. *A lonely oar floated on the tide.* To call an oar *lonely* suggests that the oar has feelings.

plot: the events of a story; what happens to the characters in a story

predict: make a reasonable guess about what will happen

setting: when and where the story happens; time and place of the story's action

short story: short work of fiction that has characters, plot, setting, and sometimes a theme

skimming: reading very quickly to get a general idea of what a text is about

speech: a talk given before an audience

summary: short review of the important information in a piece of writing

surprise ending: story ending in which the plot takes a sudden turn

text structure: the way a piece of writing is arranged. For example, short stories are written in paragraphs. Poems are written line by line.

theme: a general idea about life that an author expresses by telling a story. You can state a theme in a sentence: *Every person has the right to be free.*

verb: word that describes an action *(A stream runs through the woods)* or a state *(The water was clear and cold)*

visualize: imagine, or picture, something in your mind

Index